# 200 FARMHOUSE
## & COUNTRY HOMES

D0568403

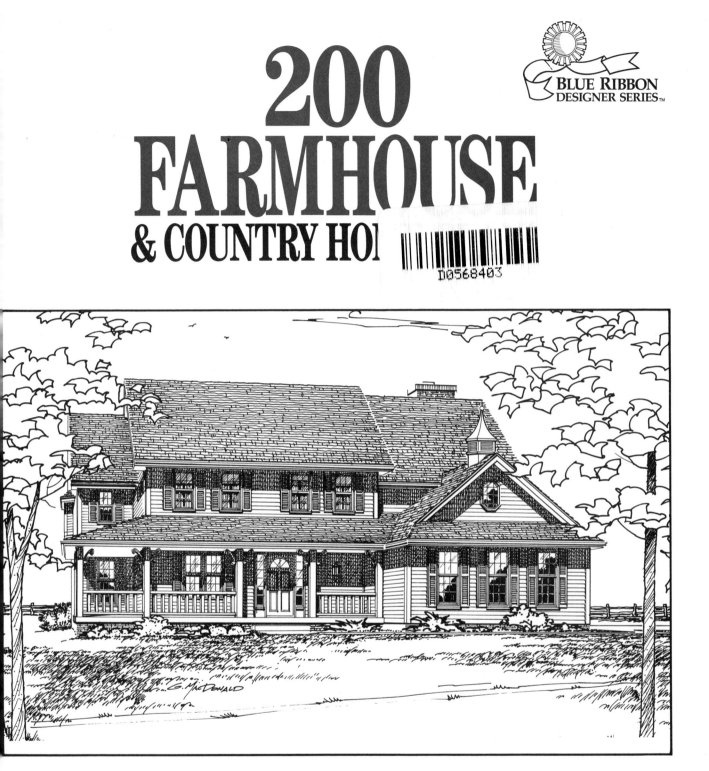

G. MacDonald

## Classic And Modern Farmhouses
## From 1299 To 4890 Square Feet

HOME PLANNERS, INC.
TUCSON, ARIZONA

**Published by Home Planners, Inc.**
Editorial and Corporate Offices:
3275 West Ina Road, Suite 110
Tucson, Arizona 85741

Distribution Center:
29333 Lorie Lane
Wixom, Michigan 48393

Rickard D. Bailey, President and Publisher
Cindy J. Coatsworth, Publications Manager
Paulette Mulvin, Editor
Paul D. Fitzgerald, Book Designer

**Photo Credits**
Front Cover: © John R. Dillon, Photographer
Back Cover: © Carl Socolow

10    9    8    7    6    5    4    3

Printed in the United States of America.

ISBN softcover: 0-918894-96-4
ISBN hardback: 1-881955-00-1

*On the front cover*: A beautifully configured Classic Farmhouse, Design Q9242,
the home of Rick and Kathy Slivka, was built by Christopher Semenza of
Semenza Homes. For additional information about this design, see page 20.

*On the back cover*: Classic Farmhouse design at its best! Our Design Q2774, the
home of John and Janie Deardorff, is a popular and practical family plan. For
more information about this design, see page 7.

# TABLE OF CONTENTS

**Editor's Note**

Everyone loves Farmhouse design—maybe because it evokes such a sense of warmth and security. From rustic exterior to cozy interior, the country style is a favorite from Mid-West plains to East and West Coast urban centers. This collection draws its inspiration from the simple honesty of country living, while actually providing the most popular features in residential housing. Filled with the spirit of the country life, this book brings together recognizable rural style and efficient, amenity-laden architectural floor planning for a selection of homes that tugs at the heart.

# About The Designers

The Blue Ribbon Designer Series™ is a collection of books featuring the home plans of a diverse group of outstanding home designers and architects known as the Blue Ribbon Network of Designers. This group of companies is dedicated to creating and marketing the finest possible plans for home construction on a regional and national basis. Each of the companies exhibits superior work and integrity in all phases of the stock-plan business including modern, trendsetting floor planning, a professionally executed blueprint package and a strong sense of service and commitment to the consumer.

## Design Basics, Inc.

For nearly a decade, Design Basics, a nationally recognized home design service located in Omaha, has been developing plans for custom home builders. Since 1987, the firm has consistently appeared in *Builder* magazine, the official magazine of the National Association of Home Builders, as the top-selling designer. The company's plans also regularly appear in numerous other shelter magazines such as *Better Homes and Gardens*, *House Beautiful* and *Home Planner*.

## Design Traditions Atlanta

Design Traditions was established by Stephen S. Fuller with the tenets of innovation, quality, originality and uncompromising architectural techniques in traditional and European homes. Especially popular throughout the Southeast, Design Traditions' plans are known for their extensive detail and thoughtful design. They are widely published in such shelter magazines as *Southern Living* magazine and *Better Homes and Gardens*.

## Alan Mascord Design Associates, Inc.

Founded in 1983 as a local supplier to the building community, Mascord Design Associates of Portland, Oregon, began to successfully publish plans nationally in 1985. With plans now drawn exclusively on computer, Mascord Design Associates quickly received a reputation for homes that are easy to build yet meet the rigorous demands of the buyers' market, winning local and national awards. The company's trademark is creating floor plans that work well and exhibit excellent traffic patterns. Their motto is: "Drawn to build, designed to sell."

## Larry W. Garnett & Associates, Inc.

Starting as a designer of homes for Houston-area residents, Garnett & Associates has been marketing designs nationally for the past ten years. A well-respected design firm, the company's plans are regularly featured in *House Beautiful*, *Country Living*, *Home* and *Professional Builder*. Numerous accolades, including several from the Texas Institute of Building Design and the American Institute of Building Design, have been awarded to the company for excellence in architecture.

## Home Planners, Inc.

Headquartered in Tucson, Arizona, with additional offices in Detroit, Home Planners is one of the longest-running and most successful home design firms in the United States. With over 2,500 designs in its portfolio, the company provides a wide range of styles, sizes and types of homes for the residential builder. All of Home Planners' designs are created with the care and professional expertise that fifty years of experience in the home-planning business affords. Their homes are designed to be built, lived in and enjoyed for years to come.

## Donald A. Gardner, Architect, Inc.

The South Carolina firm of Donald A. Gardner was established in response to a growing demand for residential designs that reflect constantly changing lifestyles. The company's specialty is providing homes with refined, custom-style details and unique features such as passive-solar designs and open floor plans. Computer-aided design and drafting technology resulting in trouble-free construction documents places the firm at the leading edge of the home plan industry.

# CLASSIC FARMHOUSES

The Classic American Farmhouse is the very essence of country-style living. It evokes images of Sunday-afternoon picnics on rolling green lawns, cold lemonade served on wide covered porches and gatherings around a cozy fireplace on wintery evenings. Its floor plans cater to family living with roomy living spaces, large kitchens and plenty of bedrooms.

Easily recognizable, the Classic Farmhouse has a number of characteristics that make it a standout. Probably most noticeable is its tall, upright, stately appearance coupled with a covered front porch or wrapping porch. The porch usually has simple, square columns with square, dimensioned railings.

The home itself is almost always two-stories, or at least 1½-stories, with the porch being either raised or at grade. The Classic Farmhouse will support a straight gabled roof that is usually steeply pitched. In some instances, the roof may have cross gables over a garage or a living area extension. It is not unusual to find a cupola or a weathervane at the rooftop or over the garage.

Covered on the exterior with horizontal wood siding, the Classic Farmhouse is trimmed with wood and sports a wood fascia. Other exterior details include a prominent chimney stack at one or both ends of the home and paned, shuttered windows in a symmetrical fenestration. Some versions may have round, half-round or Palladian windows and entry doors with fan lights. Though not common, some Classic Farmhouses have two or three dormer windows at the second floor.

Design Q2774 is the quintessential Classic Farmhouse, bringing together a rustic charm and comfortable livability. The wraparound covered porch, raised-hearth fireplace in the family room and exterior enhancements such as the shuttered, multi-pane windows and the steeply gabled roofline herald its popular interior layout. In two stories, the plan accommodates formal and informal living spaces, four bedrooms and 2½ baths. Attic space on the unfinished third floor makes a great storage area or can be developed into additional bedrooms at a later time.

This home is just one of many in the Classic Farmhouse section that draws design flavor from rustic predecessors, yet provides a comfortable, convenient home for today's family.

GARAGE
24⁰ x 21⁴

Design by
Home Planners,
Inc.

COVERED PORCH

MUD RM

DINING RM.
12⁰ x 13⁰

LIVING RM.
15⁰ x 21⁰

COUNTRY KITCHEN
16⁰ x 27⁰

CLUTTER RM
9⁰ x 9⁰

FOYER

PDR RM

MUSIC ALCOVE
9⁴ x 5⁰

LIBRARY
11⁰ x 19⁰

COVERED PORCH

65' - 8"

84' - 0"

## Design Q2694

First Floor: 2,026 square feet
Second Floor: 1,386 square feet
Total: 3,412 square feet

SEAT          SEAT

DRESSING RM          BATH          WHIRLPOOL

BEDROOM
16⁰ x 13⁴

WALK-IN CLOSET

OPEN
RAILING

MASTER BEDROOM
16⁰ x 17⁴

LINEN          BATH

BEDROOM
12⁰ x 15⁰

● This two-story design faithfully
recalls the 18th-Century homestead
of Secretary of Foreign Affairs John
Jay. California Engineered Plans and
California Stock Plans are available
for this home. Call 1-800-521-6797
for more information.

## Design Q2774

**First Floor:** 1,366 square feet
**Second Floor:** 969 square feet
**Total:** 2,335 square feet

● Another farmhouse adaptation with all the most up-to-date features expected in a new home. Beginning with the formal areas, this design offers pleasures for the entire family. There is the quiet corner living room which has an opening to the sizable dining room. This room will enjoy plenty of natural light from the delightful bay window overlooking the rear yard. It is also conveniently located with the efficient U-shaped kitchen just a step away. The kitchen features many built-ins with pass-through to the beamed-ceiling nook. Sliding glass doors to the terrace are fine attractions in both the sunken family room and nook. The service entrance to the garage has a storage closet on each side. There is extra storage in the large attic, with expansion possibilities there also. Recreational activities and hobbies can be pursued in the basement area, where there is more bulk storage space. Note four bedrooms with two baths upstairs. For information on customizing this design, call 1-800-521-6797, ext. 800. California Engineered Plans and California Stock Plans are available for this home. Call 1-800-521-6797 for more information.

Design by
Home Planners,
Inc.

7

Design by
Home Planners,
Inc.

## Design Q2946 First Floor: 1,590 square feet
Second Floor: 1,344 square feet
Total: 2,934 square feet

● This traditional farmhouse design is made for hospitality. The star attractions are the large covered porch and rear terrace, perfect gathering points for family and friends. Inside, the design offers much more: separate living room and family room, each with its own fireplace, formal dining room, large kitchen and breakfast area with bay windows, separate study with built-ins for books and other materials, workshop with plenty of room to maneuver, and mud room. The second floor offers a master suite and 3 family bedrooms plus 2 full baths. The master bedroom provides His and Hers closets with double lavatories in the master bath. For information on customizing this design, call 1-800-521-6797, ext. 800.

# Design Q3324

First Floor: 1,762 square feet
Second Floor: 1,311 square feet
Total: 3,073 square feet

● This home provides a perfect opportunity to share the comforts of traditional family living with in-home office space. The versatile plan allows for a well-positioned study off the foyer and a combination guest room/office near the laundry room—both with nearby facilities and excellent views. The large kitchen presents many possibilities for dining pleasures: a cozy meal in the breakfast nook; light eating and conversation at the bar; and evening meals in the dining room. The master bedroom provides spacious comfort with His and Hers walk-in closets and a large vanity area. The two bedrooms share a large bathroom with plenty of linen space.

Design by
Home Planners,
Inc.

## Design Q9677

First Floor: 1,584 square feet
Second Floor: 867 square feet
Total: 2,451 square feet

● Flexibility is the key to the appeal of this country-style plan. The dining room/great room can be built as one great room with the dining room relocated to the family room. The master suite has a large walk-in closet, a fireplace and a master bath with shower, whirlpool tub and double-bowl vanity. Both the sun room and master bath have access to a uniquely shaped deck. Note that there is space available on the deck for a hot tub. The screened porch offers the best in outdoor living space. Three bedrooms on the second level are joined by two full baths for convenience. Dormer windows on the second floor project out from two of the bedrooms, allowing room for window seats or storage.

Design by
Donald A.
Gardner,
Architect, Inc.

attic storage

bath

BED RM.
13-4 × 10-8

down

BED RM.
17-0 × 10-8

cl        cl        cl        cl

foyer
below

clerestory with palladian window

down

BONUS
RM.
14-4 × 23-8

Design by
Donald A.
Gardner,
Architect, Inc.

## Design Q9606

First Floor: 1,289 square feet
Second Floor: 542 square feet
Total: 1,831 square feet

● This cozy country cottage is perfect for the growing family —offering both an unfinished basement option and a bonus room. Enter through the two-story foyer with a Palladian window in a clerestory dormer above. The master suite is on the first floor for privacy and accessibility. Its accompanying bath boasts a whirlpool tub with skylight above and double-bowl vanity. The second floor contains two bedrooms, a full bath, and plenty of storage. Note that all first-floor rooms except the kitchen and utility room boast 9-foot ceilings. For crawl-space foundation, order Design Q9606; for basement foundation, order Design Q9606A.

seat

DECK
31-8 × 12-0

DINING
12-0 × 12-0

KIT.
9-0 ×
11-8

BRKFST.
9-8 × 9-8

UTILITY
10-4 × 6-4

pd.
rm.

up

storage

dry wash    cl

GARAGE
21-8 × 20-4

down

walk-in
closet

master bath

cl

GREAT RM.
13-4 × 19-4

fireplace

MASTER
BED RM.
13-4 × 13-0

up

palladian window above

PORCH
33-8 × 6-0

50-4

66-4

## Design Q3462

First Floor: 1,395 square feet
Second Floor: 813 square feet; Total: 2,208 square feet

● Get off to a great start with this handsome family farmhouse. Covered porches front and rear assure comfortable outdoor living while varied roof planes add visual interest. Inside, distinct formal and informal living zones provide the best accommodations for any occasion. The columned foyer opens to both the dining and living rooms. The central kitchen services the large family room with an island work counter and snack bar. For everyday chores, a laundry room is conveniently located and also provides access to the garage. On the first floor you'll find the master bedroom suite. It enjoys complete privacy and luxury with its double closets and master bath with double-bowl vanity, whirlpool tub and separate shower. Upstairs, three family bedrooms extend fabulous livability.

Design by
Home Planners,
Inc.

## Design Q9419

First Floor: 1,501 square feet
Second Floor: 1,341 square feet
Total: 2,842 square feet

● Totally country-styled, this home boasts a full-width porch across the front. The two-story foyer opens up to the living room on one side and through a pair of French doors to the den on the other. A large family room, nook and kitchen sweep across the back of the home over-looking the outdoor living area. An extra-large garage includes space ideal for a work bench. Four good-sized bedrooms and a large bonus room are found on the upper floor.

Design by
Alan Mascord
Design Associates, Inc.

13

## Design Q9644

First Floor: 943 square feet
Second Floor: 840 square feet
Total: 1,783 square feet

● Roundtop windows and an inviting covered porch offer an irresistible appeal for this three-bedroom plan. A two-story foyer provides a spacious feeling to this well-organized open lay-out. Round columns between the great room and kitchen add to the impressive quality of the plan. An expansive deck promotes casual outdoor living to its fullest. The master suite with walk-in closet and complete master bath is on the second floor along with two additional bedrooms and a full bath. The bonus room over the garage offers room for expansion.

Design by
Donald A. Gardner,
Architect, Inc.

# Design Q9643
First Floor: 1,165 square feet
Second Floor: 1,053 square feet
Total: 2,218 square feet
Bonus Room: 282 square feet

● The beauty of the exterior of this four-bedroom plan is enhanced by the use of arched windows, dormers and a wraparound front porch. The entrance foyer is partially open to the second level, allowing a balcony to pass over the center and generate visual excitement. Both the living and family rooms have fireplaces. The U-shaped kitchen is centrally located between the breakfast area and dining room for maximum efficiency. A large rear deck enhances outdoor living. A master suite with a generous master bath shares the second floor with three other bedrooms and a bonus room.

Design by
Donald A.
Gardner,
Architect, Inc.

**Design Q9230**

First Floor: 1,303 square feet
Second Floor: 1,084 square feet
Total: 2,387 square feet

Design by
Design
Basics,
Inc.

● It's hard to get beyond the covered front porch of this home, but doing so reveals a bright two-story entry open to the central hall. Just to the left, an enticing bay window enlivens the living room, featuring French doors which connect to the family room. The efficient kitchen with snack bar and pantry is open to the bay-windowed breakfast area with planning desk. The salad sink and counter space double as a service for the formal dining room. The master bedroom features a raised ceiling and arched window. Its adjoining bath contains a walk-through closet/transition area and a corner whirlpool.

© 1989 design basics inc.

## Design Q9214

First Floor: 1,188 square feet
Second Floor: 1,172 square feet
Total: 2,360 square feet

● Beginning with the interest of a wraparound porch, there's a feeling of country charm in this two-story plan. Formal dining and living rooms, visible from the entry, offer ample space for gracious entertaining. The large family room is truly a place of warmth and welcome with its gorgeous bay window, fireplace and French doors to the living room. The kitchen, with island counter, pantry and desk, makes cooking a delight. Upstairs, the secondary bedrooms share an efficient compartmented bath. The expansive master suite has its own luxury bath with double vanity, whirlpool, walk-in closet and dressing area.

Design by
Design
Basics,
Inc.

## Design Q9212

First Floor: 1,096 square feet
Second Floor: 975 square feet
Total: 2,071 square feet

● "Country charm" is the keynote for this delightful three-bedroom, two-story home. Create a very large great room or place a strategically located wall to provide a living room toward the front. The dining room features extra hutch space. The roomy kitchen is complete with large island counter/snack bar, pantry and desk. The gazebo-shaped breakfast room shares a through-fireplace with the great room. The three-bedroom upstairs includes a master suite which boasts an eye-catching arched transom window and bath with whirlpool.

Design by
Design
Basics,
Inc.

© 1987 design basics inc.

## Design Q9289

First Floor: 927 square feet
Second Floor: 1,163 square feet
Total: 2,090 square feet

● If you've ever dreamed of living in a country home, you'll love the wrapping porch on this four-bedroom, two-story home. Comfortable living begins in the great room with windows and nearby staircase. Just off the entry, a formal dining room was designed to make entertaining a pleasure. The large kitchen includes a pantry, island counter, roll-top desk and Lazy Susan. A private door accesses the wraparound porch from the kitchen. Be sure to take a good look at the bright dinette. Upstairs, secondary bedrooms share a centrally located bath with double vanity. For convenience, the laundry room is located on the same level as the bedrooms. The deluxe master bedroom is accessed by double doors. In the master bath, you'll enjoy the whirlpool, transom window and sloped ceiling.

Design by
**Design
Basics,
Inc.**

## Design Q9242

First Floor: 1,322 square feet
Second Floor: 1,272 square feet
Total: 2,594 square feet

● Here's the luxury you've been looking for—from the wraparound covered front porch to the bright sun room at the rear off the breakfast room. A sunken family room with fireplace serves everyday casual gatherings, while the more formal living and dining rooms are reserved for special entertaining situations. The kitchen has a central island with snack bar and is located most conveniently for serving and cleaning up. Upstairs are four bedrooms, one a lovely master suite with French doors into the master bath and a whirlpool tub in a dramatic bay window. A double vanity in the shared bath easily serves the three family bedrooms.

Design by
Design
Basics,
Inc.

Design by
Design
Basics,
Inc.

## Design Q9274

First Floor: 1,780 square feet
Second Floor: 815 square feet
Total: 2,595 square feet

● A large covered front porch welcomes visitors to this home. The entrance hall opens to a formal dining room with hutch space and a living room with built-in curio cabinets. The volume great room features a handsome fireplace flanked by windows. A large kitchen provides an island counter, pantry, dual Lazy Susans and a desk. A private hall with built-in bookcase leads to the first-floor master suite. The extravagant master bath features two walk-in closets, His and Hers vanities and a whirlpool tub. Upstairs, two of the three bedrooms feature decorator window seats.

Design by
Donald A.
Gardner,
Architect, Inc.

● Enjoy outdoor living with a covered front porch at the front of this home and an expansive deck to the rear. The floor plan allows for great livability and features split-bedroom styling with the master suite on the first floor. Upstairs bedrooms share a full bath. There is also bonus space above the garage for a studio, study or play room. For a crawl-space foundation, order Plan Q9654; for a basement foundation, order Q9654-A.

## Design Q9654

First Floor: 1,578 square feet
Second Floor: 554 square feet
Total: 2,132 square feet

DECK
34-8 × 12-0

GARAGE
20-4 × 21-8

storage

DINING
13-0 × 12-0

KIT.
10-4 × 12-0

BRKFST.
10-8 × 9-8

pd. rm.

UTIL.
dry wash

GREAT RM.
13-4 × 19-4

fireplace

walk-in closet

master bath

down

up    FOYER

MASTER
BED RM.
13-4 × 13-0

PORCH

64-0

59-0

seat    seat

cl

attic storage    attic storage

bath

BED RM.
13-4 × 10-8

BED RM.
17-0 × 10-8

down

cl    cl    cl    cl

foyer
below

clerestory with palladian window

BONUS
RM.
23-8 × 14-4

down

## Design Q9645

First Floor: 1,356 square feet
Second Floor: 542 square feet
Total: 1,898 square feet

● The welcoming charm of this country farmhouse is expressed by its many windows and its covered wraparound porch. A two-story entrance foyer is enhanced by a Palladian window in a clerestory dormer above to allow natural lighting. A first-floor master suite allows privacy and accessibility. The master bath includes a whirlpool tub, shower, and double-bowl vanity along with a walk-in closet. The first floor features a nine-foot ceiling throughout with the exception of the kitchen area, which features an eight-foot ceiling. The second floor provides two additional bedrooms, a full bath, and plenty of storage space. An unfinished basement and bonus room provide room to grow. Order Design Q9645 for crawl-space foundation; order Design Q9645-A for basement foundation.

Design by
**Donald A. Gardner, Architect, Inc.**

WIDTH 60'
DEPTH 48'

DECK

Design by
**Design Traditions**
**Atlanta**

MASTER BEDROOM
16'-0" X 16'-0"

MASTER BATH

GREAT ROOM
20'-2" X 17'-0"

BREAKFAST
11'-6" X 12'-0"

LAUNDRY

HERS    HIS

DN.

KITCHEN
13'-6" X 13'-0"

POWDER

FOYER
11'-4" X 17'-4"

UP

TWO CAR GARAGE
21'-4" X 21'-4"

DINING ROOM
15'-8" X 13'-4"

PORCH

OPEN TO BELOW

BEDROOM NO. 3
11'-8" X 12'-0"

W.I.C.

BEDROOM NO. 2
14'-4" X 12'-0"

W.I.C.

DN.

OPEN TO BELOW

BATH

BATH

BEDROOM NO. 4
13'-4" X 13'-0"

## Design Q9863 First Floor: 1,940 square feet
Second Floor: 1,025 square feet
Total: 2,965 square feet

● Some of the most charming features of Traditional design are revealed as one approaches this home. Wood siding, window shutters, flower boxes and a classic elliptical entranceway bring this architectural tradition to life. The open foyer with tray ceiling and powder room leads to the dining room. The adjacent kitchen with an octagonal counter top gives way to a spacious breakfast area with access to the deck and vaulted great room complete with fireplace. The great room hall leads to a very private master suite with bay window overlooking the back yard and easy access to the out-of-doors. The master bath with separate shower, garden tub, His and Hers vanities and a spacious walk-in closet completes the master suite. Overlooking the great room, the upper level stairway landing leads to two additional bedrooms that share a full bath. A fourth bedroom offers more privacy, with a walk-in closet and a private bath.

Design by
**Design Traditions**
Atlanta

### First Floor Plan

DECK

BREAKFAST
10'-0" X 10'-0"

TWO STORY
GREAT ROOM
14'-0" X 18'-0"

KITCHEN
12'-6" X 11'-6"

MEDIA ROOM
12'-0" X 15'-6"

UP

LAUNDRY

POWDER

DINING ROOM
12'-0" X 11'-6"

DN

UP

TWO STORY
FOYER
10'-6" X 10'-8"

LIVING ROOM
13'-4" X 10'-6"

TWO CAR GARAGE
21'-10" X 22'-0"

STOOP

### Second Floor Plan

SITTING

OPEN TO BELOW

BEDROOM NO. 2
12'-0" X 12'-0"

MASTER BEDROOM
19'-8" X 13'-6"

BALCONY

W.I.C.   W.I.C.

DN

MASTER
BATH

BATH

BEDROOM NO. 3
12'-0" X 12'-6"

OPEN TO
BELOW

W.I.C.

UNFIN. BONUS
12'-0" X 11'-4"

WIDTH 47'-0"
DEPTH 47'-6"

## Design Q9864
First Floor: 1,395 square feet
Second Floor: 1,210 square feet
Total: 2,605 square feet

● The well-balanced use of stucco and stone combined with box bay window treatments and a covered entry make this English country home especially inviting. The two-story foyer opens on the right to the attractive living and dining rooms with large windows. The step-saving kitchen and breakfast areas flow easily into the two-story great room and a media room with a see-through fireplace. The upper level offers a pleasing combination of open design and privacy. To the right of the foyer stairs, the balcony overlooks the great room. The master bedroom has a modified tray ceiling and is complete with a sitting area. The master bath with a double vanity and separate shower leads to a large walk-in closet. Double vanities are also found in the full bath off the hall. Bedrooms 2 and 3 are ample in size and feature walk-in closets. The unfinished bonus room completes this level and provides further storage space.

Design by
Home Planners,
Inc.

## Design Q2681

First Floor: 1,350 square feet
Second Floor: 1,224 square feet
Total: 2,574 square feet

● The charm of Early America is exemplified in this delightful design. Note the three areas which are highlighted by a fireplace. The three-bedroom second floor is nicely planned. Make special note of the master bedroom's many fine features. Study the rest of this design's many fine qualities.

Design by
Home Planners,
Inc.

# Design Q3325

First Floor: 1,595 square feet
Second Floor: 1,112 square feet
Total: 2,707 square feet

● Horizontal clapboard siding, varying roof planes and finely detailed window treatments set the tone for this delightful family farmhouse. The living and dining rooms function very well together. The spacious family room, with raised-hearth fireplace, and breakfast room extend a wealth of livability. Large glass doors provide an extra measure of natural illumination and direct access to the rear terrace. The U-shaped kitchen, with a tile floor, utilizes a work island supplemented by plenty of cabinet, cupboard and counter space. The sleeping accommodations of this plan include a master bedroom suite with a walk-in closet in addition to a long wardrobe closet. The master bath has a tub plus a stall shower and twin lavatories. The main bath also features twin lavatories. For information on customizing this design, call 1-800-521-6797, ext. 800.

## Design Q9314

First Floor: 1,679 square feet
Second Floor: 1,990 square feet
Total: 3,669 square feet

● Designed to be a country estate residence, this two-story home combines a sophisticated floor plan with a charming elevation. Throughout the home, beautiful windows bring the outdoors in. From the covered front porch, move inside to view a spectacular two-story entry with curving staircase. French doors lead into the library with a bayed window, built-in desk and bookcases. To the right, note the formal dining room. A great room benefits from the 10-foot spider-beamed ceiling, plus a wet bar and built-in entertainment center. Home owners will relish the combination breakfast/hearth room and kitchen concept. Upstairs, a balcony between the bedrooms overlooks the entry below. Segregation of the secondary bedrooms with walk-in closets provides privacy. Special finishing touches include the formal ceiling and bayed sitting area in the master suite. The master dressing/bath area is enhanced by His and Hers vanities, an oval whirlpool beneath the arched window and a deluxe walk-in closet with windows.

Design by
Design
Basics,
Inc.

© 1990 design basics inc.

SKYLIGHT    WHIRLPOOL

Mbr.
13⁰x16⁰

8'-4"
CEILING

BOOKS

Br.
13⁰x11¹

DN

Br.
11⁶x12⁷

OPEN TO
BELOW

Br.
13³x11⁰

STORAGE

Kt.
9⁸x13⁰

Bfst.
11⁰x12

Fam. rm.
20⁰x19⁶

DESK

BENCH

P.

Gar.
19⁸x19⁹

Dn.
12⁶x14⁰

HUTCH

BOOKS

Liv. rm.
13⁴x13⁵

UP

COVERED PORCH

41'-4"

58'-0"

© 1989 design basics inc.

## Design Q9215

First Floor: 1,386 square feet
Second Floor: 1,171 square feet
Total: 2,557 square feet

● Amenities for casual family living
and entertaining abound in this attractive
Colonial. A charming covered front
porch makes for an inviting exterior.
Inside, the two-story entry with flared
staircase opens into the formal dining
and living rooms. French doors connect
the living room with the more informal
family room for expanded entertaining
space. A spacious kitchen handily
serves both the family and dining
rooms. Also note the bay-windowed
breakfast area. The first floor features
nine-foot ceilings throughout. Upstairs
are four bedrooms, one a master suite
with a skylit bath with whirlpool and
large walk-in closet.

**Design Q2945**

First Floor: 1,644 square feet
Second Floor: 971 square feet
Total: 2,615 square feet

ATTIC 29⁴ x 26⁴ ( HEADROOM 29⁴ x 10⁴ )

BEDROOM 11⁰ x 13²

MASTER BEDROOM 13⁰ x 13²

STUDY/ BEDROOM 10⁰ x 10⁶

BEDROOM 13⁰ x 10⁰

FAMILY RM. 21⁰ x 18⁰

TERRACE

LIVING RM. 24⁰ x 13⁶

DINING RM. 13⁰ x 13⁶

BAR

LAUNDRY RM. 10⁰ x 7⁶

MUD RM.

KITCHEN 12⁰ x 13⁶

BRKFST. 9⁰ x 13⁶

GAME STOR.

FOYER

PANTRY

DESK

COVERED PORCH

GARAGE 21⁴ x 21⁸

59'-8"

54'-0"

Design by
Home Planners,
Inc.

● This masterfully affordable farmhouse manages to include all the basics— then adds a little more. Note the wraparound covered porch, large family room with raised-hearth fireplace and wet bar, spacious kitchen with island cooktop, formal dining room, and rear terrace and extra stor-age on the first floor. Upstairs, the plan's as flexible as they come: three or four bedrooms (the fourth could easily be a study or playroom) and lots of unfinished attic just waiting to be transformed into living space. This would make a fine sewing room, home office or children's play-room. Special amenities make this home a stand-out from others in its class. Note the many built-ins, the sliding glass doors to the terrace, and the wealth of closets and storage space. For information on customizing this design, call 1-800-521-6797, ext. 800.

# PLAINS OR PRAIRIE-TYPE FARMHOUSES

In the days of Western expansion, homes on the plains and prairies were, for the most part, utilitarian structures erected quickly and with little fuss. They were usually built from available materials — often sod or hay — because of the scarcity of wood or brick. Practical in form, though not especially architecturally appealing, these home were constructed to withstand the fierce winds, harsh winters and burning summer sun so prevalent in that part of the country.

Today's versions of the Plains or Prairie Farmhouse take all the best features of those sturdy ancestors and incorporate them into a much more charming and livable rendition. Their tremendous appeal derives from their nostalgic nod to pioneer beginnings and timeless endurance. Maintaining a low-slung, ground-hugging appearance (to shrug off prairie winds), the modern Prairie Farmhouse almost always has a covered front porch that wraps around at least three sides to shield the house from the sun. Some examples carry the covered porch on all four sides. This porch is usually an at-grade-level element, in keeping with the low profile of the whole house. Porch columns and railings are normally square though some turned spindles and other simple decoration may appear, echoing Colonial and Victorian influences.

The roof of these prairie homes is the most obvious design element. The entire structure of the home is dominated by a roof that is double-pitched from gable to porch covering. Looking somewhat like a large hat, these roofs function as sun-deflectors in areas of the country known for warm, dry summer seasons.

Sometimes two-story, more often 1½-story, in nature, the Prairie Farmhouse boasts upper-level dormer windows that protrude from the roof. Two or three dormer windows to a set seems to be the general rule; however, four or even five may appear on some examples. On more dramatic examples, a Palladian window may appear at the center of the second floor. The windows themselves are symmetrically set, paned and often shuttered.

Horizonal wood siding is the facing of choice, with brick and occasionally stone complementing as the exterior detailing. Chimneys generally have no regular placement but may be seen anywhere (or not at all) from the front.

Design Q9004 is a fine example of the Prairie-Type Farmhouse. Its sweeping, wide porch wraps around three sides of an exterior sided in wood and it supports a prominent roofline that is double-pitched. Three dormers grace the facade, while two chimneys (one to the left front and one to the right rear) allow for hearths throughout the house. Like others in this section, this Prairie-Type Farmhouse includes a luxurious floor plan within its rustic, countrified exterior.

## Design Q9004

First Floor: 2,166 square feet
Second Floor: 1,169 square feet
Total: 3,335 square feet

● This farmhouse design, with its expansive wraparound porch and spacious interior, will suit the needs of any large, active family. The foyer opens directly to the formal living room with an elegant fireplace. The family room offers a unique brick wall with built-in fireplace and a French door opening onto a covered porch. The well-planned kitchen overlooks a breakfast area with full-length windows that allow an uninterrupted view of the rear yard. The large utility room, with plenty of storage space, leads to an attached two-car garage. The master bedroom has access to a private study with built-in bookshelves. A third fireplace further enhances the master area. His and Hers walk-in closets, along with a garden tub and glass-enclosed shower, complete this secluded master suite. Upstairs, three bedrooms and two baths offer plenty of space and convenience for the children. A game room with an alcove that is perfect for exercise equipment provides a versatile family activity area.

Design by
Larry W.
Garnett &
Associates, Inc.

2-Car Garage

French Door

Util.

Linen

Hutches

Dining
13' x 11'-4"

Kitchen
14' x 12'

Breakfast
10' x 10'-4"

Porch

French Door

Family Room
14'-8" x 15'-4"

French Door

Bath

Linen

Master Bedroom
14'-8" x 17'

Books

Living Room
14'-4" x 19'-4"

Foyer

Books

Study
13'-4" x 10'-8"

Veranda

Width 74' - 8"
Depth 71' - 8"

Bedroom 2
16'-4" x 12'

Gameroom
17'-8" x 16'-8"

Exercise
Room

Bath 2

Bath 3

Bedroom 3
14'-4" x 11'-4"

Bedroom 4
11' x 11'-4"

## Design Q9002

First Floor: 1,504 square feet
Second Floor: 690 square feet
Total: 2,194 square feet

● The symmetry and grace of the turn-of-the-century farmhouse is captured in this design. The veranda provides plenty of shade for outdoor activities. Inside, the kitchen with center-island work counter opens to the breakfast area with a full-length bay window. The master bedroom features a walk-in closet and abundant linen storage. A corner tub and glass-enclosed shower highlight the bath. An optional French door allows access to a swimming pool, or possibly a private spa. Upstairs, the balcony overlooks the living room below. Two bedrooms each have walk-in closets and private dressing areas. Plans for a detached two-car garage are included.

Design by
Larry W.
Garnett &
Associates, Inc.

Width 57' - 4"
Depth 37' - 8"

## Design Q9000

First Floor: 1,669 square feet
Second Floor: 780 square feet
Total: 2,449 square feet

● The wraparound veranda of this farmhouse design offers a shaded outdoor living area. Inside, an efficient floor plan provides plenty of open living areas. The foyer and formal dining room are separated by a thirty-two-inch high wall, while the kitchen opens directly to a spacious breakfast area. The convenient utility room has plenty of space for a freezer and extra storage. A small rear porch can be connected by a breezeway to the de-tached garage (plans included). The highlight of this home is the living room. A center fireplace with tall glass on each side soars to the top of the cathedral ceiling, while a balcony opens from the game above. A French door opens to the rear porch. Each upstairs bedroom offers a built-in desk or window seat. The master bath features His and Hers walk-in closets and abundant linen storage.

Design by
Larry W.
Garnett &
Associates, Inc.

Width 59' - 4"
Depth 44' - 4"

# Design Q9005

First Floor: 1,995 square feet
Second Floor: 1,077 square feet
Total: 3,072 square feet

● A wraparound front porch and dormer windows give this home a casual and comfortable appearance. A leaded-glass transom above the front door, along with the dormer window in the sloped ceiling, fill the foyer with natural light. The large living area features French doors on each side of an elegant fireplace, and a built-in wet bar. An island cooktop, along with a walk-in pantry are part of the well-planned kitchen. The utility room, with extra work space, leads to an attached two-car garage and storage area. The master bedroom has generous closet space and a two-way fireplace opening into the master bath. His and Hers lavatories, an oversized tub and glass-enclosed shower complete this elegant master bath. The balcony has French doors opening into a large game room. Bedroom 3 has a private bath, while Bedroom 2 shares access to a bath with the game room. Each bedroom has a sloped ceiling and a cozy alcove created by the dormer window.

Design by
Larry W.
Garnett &
Associates, Inc.

Width 79'
Depth 60' - 6"

## Design Q3397

First Floor: 1,855 square feet
Second Floor: 1,241 square feet
Total: 3,096 square feet

Design by
**Home Planners,
Inc.**

● Five second-story dormers and a wide covered front porch add to the charm of this farmhouse design. Inside, the entry foyer opens to the left to a formal living room with fireplace and attached dining room. To the right is a private study. The back of the plan is dominated by a huge country kitchen featuring an island cook top. On this floor is the master suite with a large walk-in closet. The second floor holds three bedrooms (or two and a sitting room) with two full baths.

## Design Q3396

First Floor: 1,829 square feet
Second Floor: 947 square feet
Total: 2,776 square feet

● Rustic charm abounds in this pleasant farm-house rendition. Covered porches to the front and rear enclose living potential for the whole family. Flanking the entrance foyer are the living and dining rooms. To the rear is the L-shaped kitchen with island cook top and snack bar. A small family room/breakfast nook is attached. A private study is tucked away on this floor next to the master suite. On the second floor are three bedrooms and a full bath. Two of the bedrooms have charming dormer windows.

Design by
Home Planners,
Inc.

## Design Q3399

First Floor: 1,716 square feet
Second Floor: 2,102 square feet
Total: 3,818 square feet

Design by
**Home Planners,
Inc.**

● This is the ultimate in farmhouse living —
six dormer windows and a porch that stretches
essentially around the entire house. Inside, the
plan is open and inviting. Besides the large
country kitchen with fireplace, there is a small
game room with attached tavern, a library with
built-in bookshelves and a fireplace, and a
formal living room. The second floor has four
bedrooms and three full baths. The service
entrance features a laundry area conveniently
just off the garage.

## Design Q3398

First Floor: 1,533 square feet
Second Floor: 1,288 square feet
Total: 2,821 square feet

Design by
**Home Planners,
Inc.**

● With its classic farmhouse good-looks and just-right floor plan, this country residence has it all. The wraparound covered porch at the entry gives way to a long foyer with open staircase. To the right and left are the formal dining room and living room. More casual living areas are to the rear: a family room, and U-shaped kitchen with attached breakfast room. The second floor holds sleeping areas — two family bedrooms and a huge master suite with walk-in closet and pampering master bath.

## Design Q9067

First Floor: 1,999 square feet
Second Floor: 933 square feet
Total: 2,932 square feet

● The wraparound veranda and simple lines give this home an unassuming elegance that is characteristic of its Folk Victorian heritage. Opening directly to the formal dining room, the two-story foyer offers extra space for large dinner parties. Double French doors lead to the study with raised paneling and a cozy fireplace. Built-in bookcases conceal a hidden security vault. The private master suite features a corner garden tub, glass-enclosed shower and a walk-in closet. Overlooking the family room and built-in breakfast nook is the central kitchen. A rear staircase provides convenient access to the second floor from the family room. The balcony provides a view of the foyer below and the Palladian window. Three additional bedrooms complete this exquisite home.

9' Clg. Throughout

Design by
**Larry W. Garnett & Associates, Inc.**

REAR VIEW

WIDTH 79' 8"
DEPTH 59'

Design by
Home Planners,
Inc.

## Design Q2776
First Floor: 1,134 square feet
Second Floor: 874 square feet
Total: 2,008 square feet

● This board-and-batten farmhouse design has all of the country charm of New England. The large covered front porch will be appreciated for outdoor enjoyment. Immediately off the front entrance is the delightful corner living room. The dining room with bay window will be easily served by the U-shaped kitchen. The informal family room features a raised-hearth fireplace, sliding glass doors to the rear terrace and easy access to the powder room, laundry and service entrance. The second floor houses all of the sleeping facilities. There is a master bed- room with private bath and walk-in closet, as well as two other bedrooms sharing a full bath. This is an excellent one-and-half story design. For information on customizing this design, call 1-800-521-6797, ext. 800.

# Design Q9298

First Floor: 1,881 square feet
Second Floor: 814 square feet
Total: 2,695 square feet

● Oval windows and an appealing covered porch lend character to this 1½-story home. Inside, a volume entry views the formal living and dining rooms. Three large windows and a raised-hearth fireplace flanked by bookcases highlight a volume great room. An island kitchen with huge pantry and two Lazy Susans serves a captivating gazebo dinette. In the master suite, a cathedral ceiling, corner whirlpool and roomy dressing area deserve careful study. A gallery wall for displaying family mementos and prized heirlooms graces the upstairs corridor. Each secondary bedroom has convenient access to the bathrooms. This home's charm and blend of popular amenities will fit your lifestyle.

© design basics inc. 1991

Design by
Design
Basics,
Inc.

Design by
Design
Basics,
Inc.

Br.4
14⁰ x 12⁰

BOOKS

LIN. DN

LIN.

Br.3
13⁰ x 13⁰

OPEN
TO
BELOW

Br.2
13⁰ x 14⁰

## Design Q9297

First Floor: 2,280 square feet
Second Floor: 1,014 square feet
Total: 3,294 square feet

● Bright windows and a wraparound porch enhance the elevation of this four-bedroom, 1½-story home. Formal living and dining rooms are surveyed from the entry. A flush-hearth fireplace and transom windows highlight a volume great room planned for daily living. In the hearth room, catch a glimpse of the decorative fireplace and the convenient access to the front porch. Nearby, a sunny bayed dinette is served by an island kitchen with snack bar and two pantries. The main-floor master bedroom features a 10-foot ceiling and window seat. In the master bath, an oval whirlpool, dual vanities and walk-in closet pamper the home-owners. Upstairs, each secondary bedroom has a walk-in closet. Bedroom 3 has a private bath while Bedrooms 2 and 4 share a Hollywood bath. At 3,294 square feet, this prairie farmhouse adds distinction to any location.

Gar.
21⁴ x 29⁰

64'-0"

TRANS.        TRANS.
HEARTH

SEAT

SHELVES

Mbr.
15⁷ x 15⁰
10'-0" CEILING

Grt. rm.
20⁰ x 18⁰
10'-0" CEILING

Kit.
13⁰ x 13⁴

WHIRL
POOL

LINEN

LIN.

UP

DN

D. W.

PANT.

SNACK
BAR

P.

Bfst.
12⁰ x 12⁰

Liv. rm.
13⁰ x 13⁰

E.

Din.
13⁰ x 14⁰

TRANS.

Hrth.
13⁰ x 17⁴

WRAP AROUND PORCH

67'-4"

© design basics inc. 1991

# Design Q9603

First Floor: 1,377 square feet
Second Floor: 536 square feet
Total: 1,913 square feet

● One of the most outstanding characteristics of this plan is its flexibility — turn the great room/dining room combination into one large great room and relocate the dining room to the family room. The cheery sun room with its soothing hot tub provides access through sliding glass doors to the deck and great room and access to the master bedroom through French doors. (Don't overlook the fireplace, walk-in closet and twin vanity in the master suite.) Two second-floor bedrooms share a full bath with twin vanity and linen closet. Both bedrooms have dormer windows and walk-in closets. Other grand features include the screened porch with skylights and the sheltered front porch. For a crawlspace foundation, order plan Q9603, for a basement foundation order Q9603-A.

Design by
Donald A.
Gardner,
Architect, Inc.

## Design Q9625

First Floor: 1,436 square feet
Second Floor: 549 square feet
Sun Room: 145 square feet
Bonus Room: 334 square feet
Total: 2,319 square feet

● Great flexibility is available in this plan—the great room/dining room can be reworked into one large great room with the dining room relocated to the family room. A sun room with cathedral ceiling and sliding glass door to the deck is accessible from both the breakfast and dining rooms. A large kitchen boasts a convenient cooking island. The master bedroom has a fireplace, walk-in closet and spacious master bath. Two second-level bedrooms are equal in size and share a full bath with double-bowl vanity. Both bedrooms have a dormer window and a walk-in closet. A large bonus room over the garage is accessible from the utility room below. For a crawl-space foundation order Plan Q9625; for a basement foundation order Plan Q9625-A.

Design by
Donald A. Gardner, Architect, Inc.

# Design Q9001

First Floor: 1,308 square feet
Second Floor: 751 square feet
Total: 2,059 square feet

● A wraparound veranda and simple, uncluttered lines give this home an unassuming elegance that is characteristic of its farmhouse heritage. The kitchen overlooks an octagon-shaped breakfast room with full-length windows. The master bedroom features plenty of closet space and an elegant bath. Located within an oversized bay window is a garden tub with adjacent planter and glass-enclosed shower. Upstairs, two bedrooms share a bath with separate dressing and bathing areas. The balcony sitting area is perfect as a playroom or study. Plans for a detached two-car garage are included.

Design by
Larry W.
Garnett &
Associates, Inc.

Width 53'
Depth 45' - 4"

● Outdoor living takes a beautiful turn in this lovely home. The interior is just as great: bay windows in breakfast room and master bath, dormers and arched rear windows, sun room. The spacious great room has a fireplace, cathedral ceiling and clerestory with arched window. The master bath complements the master bedroom with a garden tub, separate shower, double-bowl vanity and walk-in closet. Two bedrooms share the upper level with a study/loft area overlooking the great room. This study area could be converted to a fourth bedroom.

## Design Q9624

First Floor: 1,659 square feet (Including Sun Room)
Second Floor: 674 square feet
Total: 2,333 square feet

Design by
Donald A. Gardner, Architect, Inc.

# Design Q9003

First Floor: 1,244 square feet
Second Floor: 551 square feet
Total: 1,795 square feet

● The timeless beauty and practicality of the wraparound veranda give this farmhouse a casual, yet distinctive appearance. The efficiently designed kitchen opens to a light-filled breakfast area with full-length windows and a French door that leads to the veranda. The master suite offers His and Hers lavatories and a large walk-in closet. Upstairs, optional skylights provide plenty of natural light to the balcony. Two bedrooms share a bath that has separate bathing and dressing areas. Plans for a two-car detached garage are included.

Width 46'
Depth 38' - 8"

Design by
**Larry W. Garnett & Associates, Inc.**

## Design Q9605

First Floor: 1,562 square feet
Second Floor: 537 square feet
Total: 2,099 square feet

● Outdoor living is realized in a wraparound covered porch at the front and sides of this house, as well as the open deck with storage to the rear. Also notice how the country feel is updated with arched rear windows and a sun room. Inside find the spacious great room with fireplace, cathedral ceiling and clerestory with arched windows. The kitchen occupies a central location between the dining room and the great room for equally convenient formal and informal occasions. A generous master suite has a fireplace and access to the sun room and covered porch. On the second level are two more bedrooms, a full bath and storage space.

Design by
Donald A.
Gardner,
Architect, Inc.

FRONT

REAR

49

**Design by**
Donald A.
Gardner,
Architect, Inc.

## Design Q9662

First Floor: 1,025 square feet
Second Floor: 911 square feet
Total: 1,936 square feet

● The exterior of this three-bedroom home is enhanced by its many gables, arched windows and wraparound porch. A large great room with impressive fireplace leads to both the dining room and screened porch with access to the deck. An open kitchen offers a country-kitchen atmosphere. The second-level master suite has two walk-in closets and an impressive bath. There is also bonus space over the garage. The plan is available with a crawl-space foundation.

# SOUTHERN OR PLANTATION-STYLE FARMHOUSES

Catering to a life filled with richness and grace, the historic homes of the Southern plantations were true showpieces. Replete with generous space for dining and entertaining, they mirrored the warm hospitality for which the South became famous. Rooms were large, ornate and filled with amenities geared toward comfort. Kitchens were the focal points around which daily life flowed. Porches, verandas and balconies were plentiful; numerous wide windows were in grand supply to catch any hint of breeze in the stifling Southern summers.

Today's Plantation-Style Farmhouse resembles the Prairie Farmhouse with its double-pitched, sprawling roofline; however, it is overall taller and more upright. The porches on these Southern belles are grand, wrapping structures that are often raised to lift the house out of wet or soggy ground. In fact, in some locations in the South, houses are built on piers to allow water to seep harmlessly beneath the level of the house. Porch columns are often round, in reminiscence of Southern Georgians or columned Colonials. The railings can be square, dimensioned lumber or round, turned spindles.

Plantation-Style homes may be either 1½ or two stories, though the most common examples are 1½-story renditions with secondary living quarters upstairs. Two-story versions may have a full, second-story balcony in the best Southern ante-bellum style. Often, secondary bedrooms are contained on the second floor with the master suite holding court on the first — a split sleeping arrangement agreeable to both children and parents.

Windows are strongly symmetrical with the second-story windows being dormers that protrude from the roof. The center unit is often larger and may have a circle-head on some more modern models. Ornate fan lights may flank entry doors.

Other exterior details include horizontal wood siding and strong, tall chimney stacks often capped with a curved masonry piece to protect the hearth from rain and spark-summoning wind. This once-only-practical design item has grown to be a style statement.

Design Q9623 incorporates some of the best details of the Southern-Style Farmhouse. Its wide covered porch extends around three sides of the design and is complemented by a beautiful deck with room for a spa to the rear. Three dormers appear at the second-story facade — the center one is a lovely Palladian-style. The characteristic protective, curved masonry piece caps the chimney which is just off center of the house. The floor plan is open and airy and contains a great room with cathedral ceiling for entertaining in high style.

Other plans in this section represent the gracious expression of Southern style. Together they provide a grand collection of homes for commodious living.

# Design Q9623

First Floor: 1,651 square feet
Second Floor: 567 square feet
Total: 2,218 square feet

● A wonderful wraparound covered porch at the front and sides of this house and the open deck with spa at the back provide plenty of outside living area. Inside, the spacious great room has a fireplace, cathedral ceiling and clerestory with arched window. The kitchen is centrally located for maximum flexibility in layout and has a food preparation island for convenience. Besides the master bedroom with access to the sun room, there are two second-level bedrooms that share a full bath. For a crawl-space foundation, order Design Q9623; for a basement foundation, order Design Q9623-A.

Design by
Donald A.
Gardner,
Architect, Inc.

Design by
Donald A.
Gardner,
Architect, Inc.

walk-in closet
lin.
master bath
bath

BED RM.
11-8 x 11-8

MASTER BED RM.
13-0 x 19-0

down

cl

cl

BED RM.
12-4 x 10-0

BED RM.
15-4 x 12-0

cl

seat

DECK

spa

PORCH

GARAGE
21-4 x 24-4

cl

UTILITY
6-8 x
12-7

d
w

KITCHEN
13-0 x 13-4

BRKFST.
9-4 x 9-10

wet bar

pd. rm.

sto.

k

FAMILY RM.
20-8 x 13-4

fireplace

DINING
13-0 x 12-8

FOYER
14-8 x 9-4

up

LIVING RM.
15-4 x 12-8

cl

cl

PORCH

80-0

57-0

## Design Q9667

First Floor: 1,357 square feet
Second Floor: 1,204 square feet
Total: 2,561 square feet

● This grand four-bedroom farmhouse with wraparound porch has eye-catching features: a double-gabled roof, Palladian window at the upper level, arched window on the lower level and intricately detailed brick chimney. Entry to the home reveals a generous foyer with direct access to all areas. The living room opens to the foyer and provides a formal entertaining area. The exceptionally large family room allows for more casual living. Look for a fireplace, wet bar and direct access to a porch and deck here. The lavish kitchen boasts a cooking island and serves the dining room, breakfast and deck areas. The master suite on the second level has a large walk-in closet and master bath with a whirlpool tub, shower and double-bowl vanity. Three additional bedrooms share a full bath.

## Design Q9632

First Floor: 1,756 square feet
Second Floor: 565 square feet
Total: 2,321 square feet

Design by
**Donald A. Gardner, Architect, Inc.**

● A wraparound covered porch at the front and sides of this house and an open deck at the back provide plenty of outside living area. The spacious great room features a fireplace, cathedral ceiling, and clerestory with an arched window. The first-floor master bedroom contains a generous closet and a master bath with garden tub, double-bowl vanity, and shower. The second floor sports two bedrooms and a full bath with double-bowl vanity. This plan includes a crawl-space foundation.

First floor plan:

- DECK
- spa
- seat
- SUN RM. 16-2 × 10-4
- skylights
- clerestory above
- BRKFST. 9-10 × 10-6
- UTIL. 8-0 × 8-6
- wash / dry
- sto.
- fireplace
- pass-thru
- GREAT RM. 15-4 × 23-2 (high ceiling)
- loft above
- KITCHEN 12-8 × 14-2
- master bath
- walk-in closet
- MASTER BED RM. 12-8 × 16-4
- sto.
- cl
- pd. rm.
- FOYER 11-10 × 7-0
- up
- DINING 14-8 × 12-4
- PORCH
- 55-0
- 59-10

Second floor plan:

- clerestory with palladian window
- bath
- lin
- walk-in closet
- great room below
- vaulted ceiling
- railing
- BED RM. 12-8 × 10-0
- cl
- bath
- cl
- down
- BED RM. 12-8 × 16-4
- LOFT/ STUDY 12-2 × 9-8
- railing
- vaulted ceiling
- foyer below
- BED RM. 12-8 × 10-0
- clerestory with palladian window

# Design Q9616

First Floor: 1,734 square feet
Second Floor: 958 square feet
Total: 2,692 square feet

● A wraparound covered porch at the front and sides of this home and the open deck with spa and seating provide plenty of outside living area. A central great room features a vaulted ceiling, fireplace and clerestory windows above. The loft/study on the second floor overlooks this gathering area. Besides a formal dining room, kitchen, breakfast room and sun room on the first floor, there is also a generous master suite with garden tub. Three second-floor bedrooms complete sleeping accommodations. The plan includes a crawl-space foundation.

Design by
Donald A.
Gardner,
Architect, Inc.

FRONT

REAR

# Design Q9621

First Floor: 1,325 square feet
Second Floor: 453 square feet
Total: 1,778 square feet

FRONT

REAR

● For the economy-minded family desiring a wraparound covered porch, this compact design has all the amenities available in larger plans with little wasted space. In addition, a front Palladian window, dormer and rear arched windows provide exciting visual elements to the exterior. The spacious great room has a fireplace, cathedral ceiling and clerestory arched windows. A second-level balcony overlooks this gathering area. The kitchen is centrally located for maximum flexibility in layout and features a pass-through to the great room. Besides the generous master suite with well-appointed full bath, there are two family bedrooms located on the second level sharing a full bath with double vanity. Note the ample attic storage space. For a crawl-space foundation, order Design Q9621; for a basement foundation, order Design Q9621-A.

Design by
Donald A.
Gardner,
Architect, Inc.

## Design Q9668

First Floor: 1,254 square feet
Second Floor: 1,060 square feet
Total: 2,314 square feet

Design by
Donald A.
Gardner,
Architect, Inc.

● This stylish country farmhouse shows off its good looks both front and rear. A wraparound porch allows sheltered access to all first-level areas along with a covered breezeway to the garage. On the first floor, the spacious, open layout has all the latest features. The master bedroom on the second level has a fireplace, large walk-in closet and a master bath with shower, whirlpool tub and double-bowl vanity. Three additional bedrooms share a full bath with double-bowl vanity.

## Design Q3510

First Floor: 1,120 square feet
Second Floor: 1,083 square feet
Third Floor: 597 square feet
Total: 2,800 square feet

● From the front and back covered porches to the open foyer with dining and living rooms on each side, this Colonial home offers a glimpse of the Old South. The large kitchen features an island cooktop, a breakfast nook and a convenient planning desk. The master bedroom exudes Southern flair with a spacious bathroom and a separate make-up table. An additional third-floor bonus room is also available. Fireplaces in the dining room, the living room and the family room complete the warmth and vitality of this fine home. All in all, it will serve your family well for generations to come.

Design by
**Home Planners, Inc.**

Design by
Home Planners,
Inc.

## Design Q3570

First Floor: 1,578 square feet
Second Floor: 1,546 square feet
Total: 3,124 square feet
Bonus Room: 380 square feet

● The unique design of this Colonial will satisfy the most refined tastes. Well-designed traffic patterns define family and formal areas. But that doesn't mean all the amenities are left for company. For example, the family room and its fireplace create a warm atmosphere for playing a board game with the kids or just relaxing. The kitchen features an island cooktop and a view onto the back porch. The roomy first-floor laundry includes space for drip drying. If it's not laundry day then take in the good weather from the second-floor balcony or slip into the master bath's whirlpool. With an additional three bedrooms and two bathrooms as well as a large bonus room above the garage, your family will have plenty of room to grow.

## Design Q2981

First Floor: 2,104 square feet
Second Floor: 2,015 square feet
Total: 4,119 square feet

Design by
**Home Planners, Inc.**

● This formal two-story recalls a Louisiana plantation house, Land's End, built in 1857. The Ionic columns of the front porch and the pediment gable
echo the Greek Revival style. Highlighting the interior is the bright and cheerful spaciousness of the
informal family room area. It features a wall of
glass stretching to the second story sloping ceiling.
Enhancing the drama of this area is the adjacent
glass area of the breakfast room. Note the
"His/Her" areas of the master bedroom.

# Design Q3508

First Floor: 2,098 square feet
Second Floor: 1,735 square feet
Total: 3,833 square feet

● Make history with this modern version of Louisiana's "Rosedown House." Like its predecessor—built in the 1800s—the modern adaptation exhibits splendid Southern styling, but with today's most sought-after amenities. The formal zone of the house is introduced by a foyer with a graceful, curving staircase. The dining and living rooms flank the foyer—each is highlighted by a fireplace. Off the living room, a library or music room offers comfort with a corner fireplace and a covered porch. This room also accesses the family room where more informal living takes off with a nearby breakfast room, expansive kitchen and rear covered porch. Upstairs, three bedrooms (one with its own bath) and a study (which may convert to an additional bedroom, if desired) include a gracious master suite. It opens with double doors and furthers this romantic feeling with a fireplace. A large dressing room with walk-in closets leads to the luxury bath. Two covered balconies complete the superb livability found in this plan.

Width 95'-4"
Depth 48'-8"

Design by
Home Planners,
Inc.

## Design Q9850

First Floor: 1,960 square feet
Second Floor: 905 square feet
Total: 2,865 square feet

Design by
**Design Traditions**
Atlanta

BEDROOM NO.2
14'-0" X 11'-0"

OPEN TO BELOW

UNFINISHED STORAGE
7'-10" X 12'-2"

DN.

BATH

BEDROOM NO.3
13'-10" X 12'-0"

BATH

BEDROOM NO.4
12'-4" X 12'-0"

DECK

BREAKFAST
13'-4" X 8'-0"

UP

GREAT ROOM
19'-0" X 14'-0"

MASTER BEDROOM
13'-4" X 20'-2"

W.I.C.

KITCHEN
14'-0" X 14'-2"

DN.

POWDER

MASTER BATH
10'-0" X 15'-0"

LAUNDRY
6'-0" X 9'-10"

DINING ROOM
13'-10" X 12'-0"

FOYER
7'-0" X 12'-0"

LIVING ROOM
13'-10" X 12'-0"

STORAGE

TWO CAR GARAGE
21'-4" X 22'-0"

PORCH

Width 69'-8"
Depth 59'

● This Georgian country-style home displays an impressive appearance. Textures of brick and wood are used to reflect this architectural period perfectly. Georgian symmetry balances the living room and dining room to the right and left of the foyer. Both are framed by columns, while the living room features its own fireplace. The main level continues into the two-story great room with built-in cabinetry, fireplace, and a large bay window that overlooks the rear deck. A powder room is conveniently located next to the living room. A dramatic tray ceiling, a wall of glass and access to the rear deck complete the master bedroom. The master bath features separate vanities and a large walk-in closet. Left of the great room, the main level includes a large kitchen that opens to the breakfast area and staircase. Upstairs are three bedrooms and an open railing overlooking the great room below. Each bedroom features ample closet space and direct access to a bathroom.

Copyright 1992 Stephen S. Fuller, Inc.

# Design Q9851

First Floor: 2,210 square feet
Second Floor: 1,070 square feet
Total: 3,280 square feet

● A generous front porch enhances the living area of this home with its sheltering welcome and Americana detailing. The classic style is also echoed in the use of wood siding, shuttered windows and stone finish work on two chimneys. The main level begins with a two-story foyer with tray ceiling.

Double doors open into the study with an exposed beam ceiling and fireplace. Left of the foyer lies the dining room drenched in natural sunlight. Across the hall, the great room with fireplace, wet bar and two sets of French doors provides a great gathering place. A hall powder room is to the right rear of the foyer. The master suite is located at the end of the main hallway. It features a tray ceiling and a complete master bath with separate shower, walk-in closet and dual vanities. The two-car garage is at the rear of the home, with convenient access from the expansive kitchen and breakfast area. Staircases from the family room and foyer lead to the upper level. Two additional bedrooms, each having walk-in closets and vanities, share the tub area. A third bedroom has a generous walk-in closet and private bath.

Design by
**Design Traditions**
Atlanta

## Design Q9669

First Floor: 1,759 square feet
Second Floor: 888 square feet
Total: 2,647 square feet

● This complete four-bedroom country farmhouse ignites a passion for both indoor and outdoor living with the well-organized open layout and the continuous flowing porch and deck encircling the house. Front and rear Palladian window dormers allow natural light to penetrate the foyer and family room below as well as adding exciting visual elements to the exterior. The dramatic family room with sloped ceiling envelopes a curved balcony. The master suite includes a large walk-in closet, a special sitting area, and a master bath with whirlpool tub, shower and double bowl vanity. A bonus room over the garage adds to the completeness of this house.

Design by
Donald A. Gardner, Architect, Inc.

Design by
**Larry W.
Garnett &
Associates, Inc.**

## Design Q9087
First Floor: 2,263 square feet
Second Floor: 787 square feet
Total: 3,050 square feet

● Excellent outdoor living is yours with this 1½-story home. The wrapping covered front porch gives way to a center hall entry with flanking living and dining rooms. The living room features a media center, two-way fireplace and columned entry. The attached garden room has French doors to the front porch and French doors to a smaller covered porch that is also accessed through the master bedroom suite. The family room is complemented by a fireplace, built-in bookshelves and another covered porch. An angled island counter separates it from the kitchen. Upstairs are three bedrooms and two full baths. Bedroom 4 has a beautiful bumped out window while Bedrooms 2 and 3 have dormer windows.

**Bedroom 4**
13' x 14'-8"

Balcony

**Bath 2**

**Bath 3**

**Bedroom 2**
11'-4" x 12'

**Bedroom 3**
11'-4" x 12'

Porch

**Breakfast**
9'-4" x 10'

Util.

Linen

**Bath**

**Master Bedroom**
19'-4" x 17'

French Door

Porch

French Door

Books

**Family Room**
13'-4" x 13'-4"

**Kitchen**
12' x 12'

1/2 Bath

Media Center

French Door

**Living Room**
14'-8" x 20'

**Garden Room**
12'-4" x 13'

**Dining**
15'-4" x 11'-4"

Foyer

2-Way Fireplace

French Door

Porch

**Living Room**

Width 68'-10"
Depth 52'-4"

Design by
Home Planners,
Inc.

## Design Q2996

First Floor: 2,191 square feet
Second Floor: 1,928 square feet
Total: 4,119 square feet

● Covered porches upstairs and down are a charming addition to the well appointed two-story. Four chimney stacks herald four hearths inside: living room, dining room, family room and study. The second floor holds four bedrooms including a master suite with its own fireplace and a huge walk-in closet.

## Design Q3567

First Floor: 1,778 square feet
Second Floor: 1,663 square feet
Bonus Room: 442 square feet
Total: 3,883 square feet

● Spring breezes and summer nights will be a joy to take in on the verandas and balcony of this gorgeous Southern Colonial. Or, if you prefer, sit back and enjoy a good book in the library, or invite an old friend over for a chat in the conversation room. The first floor also includes formal dining and living rooms, a service entry with laundry and a three-car garage. You'll find a bonus room over the garage; you may decide to turn it into a media room or an exercise room. The master bedroom sports a fireplace, two walk-in closets, a double-bowl vanity, a shower and a whirlpool tub. Three other bedrooms occupy the second floor; one has its own full bath. Of course, the balcony is just a step away.

Design by
Home Planners,
Inc.

## Design Q2991

First Floor: 2,658 square feet
Second Floor: 1,429 square feet
Total: 4,087 square feet

Design by
Home Planners,
Inc.

● This antebellum Greek Revival manor represents the grace of Southern plantation style. Between covered front and rear verandas lies a floor plan for great livability. Flanking a wide entry foyer are the formal living and dining rooms. Each has its own fireplace. Less formal activities take place in the family room which is conveniently open to the island kitchen. A handy cook top with snack bar island serves both areas. Separating living areas from the master suite is a quiet study. On the second floor are three bedrooms and three full baths. There's also a small sitting room and a storage area.

# VICTORIAN-INFLUENCED FARMHOUSES

In a time defined by freedom of expression, the Romantic ideals of architecture helped bring about Victorian style. For 70 years, from 1840 to 1910, people embraced the style and developed its various shapes and forms. So popular were the features of Victoriana that many of its more prominent, ornate characteristics began appearing on otherwise plain facades. Simple, unadorned farmhouses were seen sporting Queen-Anne-Style porch rails and posts, decorative corner brackets, spindlework friezes and other "gingerbread" details. This was possible (and practical) because of the availability of pre-cut Victorian trim pieces obtained through local lumber yards. The long-lasting appeal of Victorian detailing is evident, as the features appear on myriads of homes built throughout the country.

The Victorian Farmhouse today presents many of the same properties as the Classic Farmhouse — tall, upright proportions with wood siding and covered porches. However, the Victorian era influenced these rural residences by enhancing the plainness of Farmhouse style with detailing. Special features that became part of this newly integrated design include round or square double porch columns, spindled railings and friezes, spiderweb decoration at gables, shingle scallops, and cornice and dentil ornamentation.

Structural modifications were also accomplished to the basic Farmhouse design that make these simpler homes much more appealing. Plain, symmetrical windows became metal-clad, French-style bays or dormer windows. Even circle-head and fan-type windows were added. Wings and appendages were attached and took the shape of hexagons or octagons. Shingles took the place of horizontal wood siding in many instances.

In the following collection of Victorian Farmhouses, two designs are able representatives of the style: Design Q9015 and Design Q2970. Though obviously descended from stolid farmhouse roots, Design Q9015 is a model of exquisite detailing. Turned posts and delicate spindles adorn the covered front porch; eave brackets and lacy cornice trim grace the exterior. Of special note is the metal-clad roof over the porch and the decorative work on the pediments at the dormer windows. Design Q2970 presents many of the same details and also adds shingle scallops and a hexagonal bump-out that holds the dining room on the first floor and a sitting room on the second floor.

Displayed in both one- and two-story versions, the Victorian Farmhouses in this section are filled with the charm and delight that has always made Victorian styling so popular.

## Design Q9420

First Floor: 1,587 square feet
Second Floor: 716 square feet
Bonus Room: 427 square feet
Total: 2,730 square feet

Design by
**Alan Mascord**
Design Associates, Inc.

◀ 54' ▶

▲
49'
▼

● This compact Victorian home has its fully featured master bedroom on the main floor. A wraparound porch with a pair of French doors leading from the dining room complements the facade. The upper hallway overlooks the vaulted family room on one side and the two-story foyer on the other. A bonus room over the garage allows some expansion space to either add another bedroom or a game room.

Design by
**Alan Mascord
Design Associates, Inc.**

◀ 49' ▶

▲
47'
▼

VAULTED
FAMILY
13/0 X 13/6

NOOK
9/6 X 13/6

8/6 X 13/6

GARAGE
21/8 X 21/4

DESK

D. W.

DINING
10/8 X 12/0 +

UP

PARLOR
13/0 X 11/10 +

## Design Q9475

First Floor: 1,085 square feet
Second Floor: 1,110 square feet
Total: 2,195 square feet

● Farmhouse design is popular throughout the country—this plan is an outstanding example. The corner entry leads to a formal parlor on the left and dining room on the right. To the rear of the first floor are the family room with fireplace and island kitchen with nook. The stairs are centrally located and a nearby powder room will be appreciated by guests. Upstairs are four bedrooms (or three and a den). The master bedroom has a vaulted ceiling and lovely private bath.

SPA

VAULTED
MASTER
12/0 X 15/8

LINEN

DEN /
BR. 4
10/8 X 12/0

BR. 2
10/8 X 11/2

DN.

BR. 3
13/0 X 11/10

## Design Q9054

First Floor: 860 square feet
Second Floor: 818 square feet
Total: 1,678 square feet

● Taking its cue from Victorian design, this two-story home allows for a great deal of livability in a smaller square footage. Downstairs are the living and dining areas, plus full work areas in a galley kitchen, utility room, and powder room. The wraparound veranda provides lovely indoor/outdoor living potential. Upstairs are three bedrooms with large closets. The master bedroom has a bay window and bath with double-bowl vanity. Secondary bedrooms share a full bath. Thoughtful extras like the fireplace in the living room, coat closet in the foyer and dividing wall between the living room and dining room make this a very special plan.

Design by
Larry W.
Garnett &
Associates, Inc.

WIDTH 37'
DEPTH 33'-10"

French Doors

Master Bedroom
13'-4" x 17'
11' Clg.

Bath

Breakfast
8' x 8'

Kitchen
16' x 12'

Bath 2

French Door

Bedroom 3
12' x 12'
11' Step-Up Clg.

Util.

Dining
15'-8" x 10'-8"
12' Clg.

Raised
Foyer

Bedroom 2
13' x 11'-4"

French
Doors

Living Room
21' x 14'-4"
12' Clg.

Veranda

Width 50'-4"
Depth 58'

Bath 3

Plant Shelves

Foyer Below

Gameroom
18'-8" x 15'-4"

Design by
Larry W.
Garnett &
Associates, Inc.

## Design Q9030

First Floor: 1,837 square feet
Second Floor: 445 square feet
Total: 2,282 square feet

● A seven-foot wide veranda with ornate fretwork, porch railing and intricate post brackets, along with a copper-topped box window provide this home with old-fashioned charm and romance. Inside, the raised foyer opens into living and dining areas that are perfect for family activities or formal entertaining. Stairs lead to the second floor gameroom and bath. Bedrooms 2 and 3 each have French doors that open to the front veranda. The secluded master bedroom has an eleven-foot ceiling and French doors, while the spacious master bath features a garden tub with adjacent glass-enclosed shower, along with a large walk-in closet. The kitchen combines both form and function with ample cabinet space, a center work island, and a magnificent view through the breakfast area to the rear yard. Plans for a detached two-car garage are included with this design.

## Design Q3384 First Floor: 1,399 square feet
Second Floor: 1,123 square feet
Total: 2,522 square feet

● Classic Victorian styling comes to the forefront in this Queen Anne two-story. Complementary fishscale-adorned pediments top the bayed tower to the left and garage to the right. Smaller versions are found at the dormer windows above a spindlework porch. The interior boasts comfortable living quarters for the entire family. On opposite sides of the wide foyer are the formal dining and living rooms. To the rear, is a country-style island kitchen with attached family room (don't miss the fireplace here). A small library shares a covered porch with this informal gathering area and also has its own fireplace. T bedrooms on the second floor includ master suite with grand bath. The tw ily bedrooms share a full bath. Take note of the service area conveniently attached to the two-car garage.

Design by
Home Planners,
Inc.

## Design Q3385

First Floor: 1,096 square feet
Second Floor: 900 square feet
Total: 1,996 square feet

● Covered porches front and rear
are the first signal that this is a fine
example of Folk Victorian styling.
Complementing the exterior is a
grand plan for family living. A formal living room and attached dining
room provide space for entertaining
guests. The large family room with
fireplace is a gathering room for
everyday. Both areas have access to
outdoor spaces. Four bedrooms
occupy the second floor. The master
suite features two lavatories, a window seat and three closets. One of
the family bedrooms has its own private balcony and could be used as a
study. Note the open staircase and
convenient linen storage.

Design by
Home Planners,
Inc.

## Design Q3461

First Floor: 1,391 square feet
Second Floor: 611 square feet
Total: 2,002 square feet

● A Palladian window set in a dormer provides a nice introduction to this 1½-story country home. The two-story foyer draws on natural light and a pair of columns to set a comfortable, yet elegant mood. The living room, to the left, presents a grand space for entertaining. From full-course dinners to family suppers, the dining room will serve its purpose well. The kitchen delights with an island work station and openness to the keeping room. Here, a raised-hearth fireplace provides added comfort. Sleeping accommodations are comprised of four bedrooms, one a first-floor master suite. With a luxurious private bath, including dual lavatories, this room will surely be a favorite retreat. Upstairs, three secondary bedrooms meet the needs of the growing family.

Design by
Home Planners,
Inc.

## Design Q3307

First Floor: 1,765 square feet
Second Floor: 1,105 square feet
Total: 2,870 square feet

● This charming design brings together the best in historical styling and modern floor planning. Inside, the first-floor plan boasts formal living and dining areas on either side of the entry foyer, a study that could double as a guest room, a large family room with raised-hearth fireplace and snack bar pass-through, and a U-shaped kitchen with attached breakfast room. Two family bedrooms on the second floor share a full bath; the master bedroom has a thoughtfully appointed bath and large walk-in closet.

Design by
Home Planners,
Inc.

## Design Q9854

Square Footage: 2,770

● This English cottage with cedar shake exterior displays the best qualities of a traditional design. With the bay window and recessed entry visitors feel warmly welcomed. The foyer opens to both the dining room with vaulted ceiling and great room with fireplace and built-in cabinetry. Surrounded by windows, the breakfast room opens to a gourmet kitchen and laundry room conveniently located near the garage entrance. To the right of the foyer is a hall powder room. Two bedrooms with large closets are joined by a full bath with individual vanities and window seat. Through double doors at the end of a short hall, the master suite awaits with tray ceiling and adjoining sunlit sitting room. The master bath has His and Hers closets, separate vanities, individual shower and a garden tub with bay window.

Design by
**Design Traditions**
Atlanta

**DECK**

**SITTING**
12'- 0"x 12'- 0"

W.I.C.

**MASTER
BATH**

**BREAKFAST**
12'- 0"x 13'- 6"

DN.

**GREAT ROOM**
20'- 6"x 18'- 6"

**MASTER SUITE**
16'- 6"x 15'- 0"

W.I.C.

**KITCHEN**
14'-3"x 13'- 6"

**POWDER**

**BEDROOM NO.3**
12'- 0"x 12'- 0"

**FOYER**

**LAUNDRY**
9'-0" X 8'-6"

**DINING ROOM**
13'-6" X 14'-6"

**BEDROOM NO.2**
12'- 3"x 14'- 0"

**BATH**

**STOOP**

**STORAGE**

**TWO CAR GARAGE**
21'- 6"x 27'- 6"

Width 73'-6"
Depth 78'

Copyright 1992 Stephen S. Fuller, Inc.

Design by
**Design Traditions**
**Atlanta**

MASTER
BATH

PORCH

MASTER BEDRDOOM
16'-4" X 13'-6"

BEDROOM/
OFFICE
10'-4" X 11'-0"

BREAKFAST
13'-4" X 9'-0"

GREAT ROOM
17'-0" X 17'-8"

BEDROOM NO. 2
10'-4" X 12'-0"

KITCHEN
13'-4" X 10'-6"

DN.

BATH

LAUNDRY

BATH

TWO CAR GARAGE
20'-6" X 19'-6"

DINING ROOM
11'-4" X 12'-10"

FOYER
5'-4" X
12'-10"

BEDROOM/
STUDY
11'-2" X 12'-0"

PORCH

Width 61'
Depth 70'-6"

## Design Q9853
Square Footage: 2,090

● This traditional home features board and batten and cedar shingles in an attractively proportioned exterior. Finishing touches include a covered entrance and porch with column detailing and arched transom, flower boxes and shuttered windows. The foyer opens to both the dining room and great room beyond with French doors opening onto the porch. Through the double doors to the right of the foyer is the combination bedroom/study. A short hallway leads to a full bath and a secondary bedroom with ample closet space. The master bedroom is spacious, with walk-in closets on both sides of the entrance to the master bath. With separate vanities, shower and toilet, the master bath is of symmetrical design, and forms a private retreat at the rear of the home. Convenient to both the great room and dining room, the kitchen opens to an attractive breakfast area featuring a bay window. An additional room is remotely located off the kitchen, providing a retreat for today's at-home office or guest.

## Design Q9852

First Floor: 1,840 square feet
Second Floor: 950 square feet
Total: 2,790 square feet

Design by
**Design Traditions**
Atlanta

● The appearance of this early American home brings the past to mind with its wraparound porch, wood siding and flower-box detailing. The uniquely shaped foyer leads to the dining room accented by columns, vaulted ceiling and bay window. Columns frame the great room as well, while a ribbon of windows creates a wall of glass at the back of the house from the great room to the breakfast area. The asymmetrical theme continues through the kitchen as it leads back to the hallway, accessing the laundry and two-car garage. Left of the

foyer lies the living room with a warming fireplace. The master suite begins with double doors that open to a space with octagonal tray ceiling and bay window. The spacious master bath and walk-in closet complete the suite. Stairs to the second level lead from the breakfast area to an open landing overlooking the great room. Three additional bedrooms with large walk-in closets and a variety of bath arrangements complete this level.

WIDTH 58'-6"
DEPTH 62'

Copyright 1992 Stephen S. Fuller, Inc.

## Design Q9868

First Floor: 1,725 square feet
Second Floor: 650 square feet
Total: 2,375 square feet

● This example of Classic American architecture features a columned front porch and wood framing. Bay window detailing and an arched dormer above the porch complete the picture. The foyer includes a closet and an open staircase to the upper level. Straight ahead, the great room is largely glass, and opens to the vaulted breakfast area which leads outdoors to the patio. The octagonal kitchen is designed for ease of movement and to promote the flow of family traffic. The dining room and living room share a hearth and an open design with bay window treatments for interest and natural light. The master bedroom at the right rear of the home features a tray ceiling and large bay window. The master bath with dual vanities, individual shower and walk-in closets completes the master suite. The upper level is comprised of a gallery and loft open to the great room and foyer below, which is warmed by the natural light from the dormer windows. Beyond the loft are two bedrooms that share a bath and an unfinished bonus room. Upper level attic storage is spacious and convenient with an entrance just at the top of the stairs.

WIDTH 60'-6"
DEPTH 50'-6"

Design by
Design Traditions
Atlanta

Copyright 1991 Stephen S. Fuller, Inc.

## Design Q9232

First Floor: 1,551 square feet
Second Floor: 725 square feet
Total: 2,276 square feet

● This narrow-lot plan features a wraparound porch at the two-story entry, which opens to the formal dining room with beautiful bay windows. The great room features a handsome fireplace and a ten-and-a-half foot ceiling. A well-equipped island kitchen with pantry and built-in desk is available for the serious cook. The large master bedroom has a vaulted ceiling and a luxury master bath with two-person whirlpool, skylight and large walk-in closet. Three secondary bedrooms with ample closet space share a compartmented bath including double vanity and a large linen closet.

Design by
**Design Basics, Inc.**

© 1989 design basics inc.

## Design Q9252

First Floor: 1,113 square feet
Second Floor: 965 square feet
Total: 2,078 square feet

● Elegant detail, a charming veranda and a tall brick chimney make a pleasing facade on this four-bedroom, two-story Victorian home. Yesterday's simpler lifestyle is reflected throughout this plan. From the large bayed parlor with sloped ceiling to the sunken gathering room with fireplace, there's plenty to appreciate about the floor plan. The formal dining room opens to the parlor for convenient entertaining. An L-shaped kitchen with attached breakfast room is nearby. Upstairs quarters include a master suite with private dressing area and whirlpool, and three family bedrooms.

Design by
**Design
Basics,
Inc.**

# Design Q9008

First Floor: 1,653 square feet
Second Floor: 613 square feet
Total: 2,266 square feet

● While much less elaborate than other Victorian styles, the intersecting roof lines, arch-top windows with shutters, and detailed corner pilasters give this home a casual, yet distinctive appearance. An eight-foot-wide veranda provides plenty of room for outdoor entertaining. Inside, the large foyer opens to the formal dining area. A thirteen-foot raised ceiling with blocked panel trim and crown molding adds interest to the living room. French doors lead to a private library with built-in bookcases and a window seat. The secluded master suite offers a walk-in closet and an elegant bath with garden tub and glass-enclosed shower. Upstairs, the balcony features a built-in bookcase. Two large bedrooms each have walk-in closets and ceilings that slope from six feet to nine feet in height. Plans for a detached garage are included.

2-Car Garage

Bedroom 2
12'-4" x 13'

6' Wall

Balcony

Books

6' Wall

Bedroom 3
11' x 14'

Bath 2

Linen

Linen

Bath

French Doors

Master Bedroom
14'-4" x 16'

Porch

French Door

Util.

Breakfast
10' x 9'

Kitchen
11'-4" x 11'-4"

French Door

Living Room
17'-8" x 17'
13' Step-Up Clg.

Dining
11'-4" x 13'-4"

Foyer

French Doors

Porch

Library
10'-8" x 11'
10' Clg.

Window Seat
Books

Design by
Larry W.
Garnett &
Associates, Inc.

Width 54'
Depth 53' - 8"

Bedroom 4
12'-4" x 13'-4"

Bedroom 3
13'-8" x 13'-4"
11' Clg.

Laundry Chute

Bath 2

42" High Wall

Bedroom 2
15'-4" x 11'-4"
Cathedral Clg.

2-Car Garage

Util.

Linen  Bath

Breakfast
8' x 8'

Hamper

Master Bedroom
13'-8" x 13'-4"

Kitchen

French Door

French Door

Dining
10' x 12'-8"
13' Clg.

Gallery

Foyer

French Door

Living Room
15'-4" x 16'

WIDTH 46'-8"
WIDTH w/Piazza 58'-4"
DEPTH 72'-4"

Piazza

Veranda

Design by
Larry W.
Garnett &
Associates, Inc.

## Design Q9009

First Floor: 1,351 square feet
Second Floor: 862 square feet
Total: 2,213 square feet

● The most distinctive characteristic of the Queen Anne style, the steeply pitched hipped central roof with cross gables, is evident on this design. Inside, the dining room and living room offer magnificent views. A breakfast alcove is part of the efficient kitchen. French doors and a bay window provide a comfortable retreat in the secluded master suite. Three additional bedrooms are found upstairs.

## Design Q9053 First Floor: 811 square feet; Second Floor: 1,067 square feet; Total: 1,878 square feet

● Elaborate spindlework and ornate porch posts, along with detailed block-paneled trim at the symmetrical gables, give this Queen Anne Style two-story charm and elegance. The living room has a fireplace as its focal point, while at the same time providing a view of the built-in media center. The large kitchen opens to the dining area, and also has access to the garage and laundry room. The master bedroom is truly a luxurious private retreat. The sitting area has a built-in media center for audio and video equipment. The master bath contains a glass-enclosed shower and His and Hers lavatories. Two additional bedrooms, each with a walk-in closet, share a hall bath.

Width 45'
Depth 53'

2-Car Garage

Porch

French Door

Util.

Kitchen
10' x 12'

Stor.

Dining
10' x 10'

1/2 Bath

Media Center

Foyer

Living Room
15' x 18'-8"

Veranda

9' Clg. Throughout First and Second Floors

Books

Bath
2

Bedroom 2
12'-8" x 11'-4"

Bedroom 3
10' x 11'-8"

Media Center

Sitting Area
9'-8" x 10'

Balcony

Bath

Master Bedroom
15' x 18'-8"

Design by
Larry W.
Garnett &
Associates, Inc.

Width 59' - 4"
Depth 72' - 8"

Design by
**Larry W. Garnett & Associates, Inc.**

## Design Q9015

First Floor: 1,948 square feet
Second Floor: 1,891 square feet
Total: 3,839 square feet

● As authentic as the exterior of this design is, the interior offers all the luxury and elegance that today's homeowners could desire. The formal living and dining rooms are separated by detailed wood columns. Built-in bookcases and cabinets highlight the block-paneled study. The centrally located kitchen becomes the focal point of a truly outstanding family living center which includes a sunken media area, breakfast alcove, and a family room with a fireplace. Adjacent to the kitchen is a large hobby room with a built-in desk, a space for a freezer, and generous cabinet storage. A rear staircase provides convenient access to the second floor. The secluded master suite is beyond compare, with such extras as a fireplace with flanking window seats and cabinets, an enormous walk-in closet, and a private deck. The luxurious bath features a dressing table, a whirlpool tub with a gazebo-shaped ceiling above, and an oversized shower. Finally, there is a private exercise room with a bay-window seat. Three additional bedrooms and a laundry room complete the second floor. A staircase leads to an optional third floor area.

## Design Q2970 First Floor: 1,538 square feet
Second Floor: 1,526 square feet; Third Floor: 658 square feet
Total: 3,722 square feet

● A porch, is a porch, is a porch. But, when it wraps around to a side, or even two sides, of the house, we have called it a veranda. This charming Victorian features a covered outdoor living area on all four sides! It even ends at a screened porch which features a sun deck above. This interesting plan offers three floors of livability. And what livability it is! Plenty of formal and informal living facilities to go along with the potential of five bedrooms. The master suite is just that. It is adjacent to an interesting sitting room. It has a sun deck and excellent bath/personal care facilities. The third floor will make a wonderful haven for the family's student members.

Design by
Home Planners,
Inc.

# Design Q2974

First Floor: 911 square feet
Second Floor: 861 square feet; Total: 1,772 square feet

● Victorian homes are well known for their orientation on narrow building sites. This house is 38 feet wide, but the livability is tremendous. From the front covered porch, the foyer directs traffic all the way to the back of the house with its open living and dining rooms. The U-shaped kitchen conveniently services both the dining room and the front breakfast room. The rear living area is spacious and functions in an exciting manner with the outdoor areas. Bonus recreational, hobby and storage is offered by the basement and the attic. California Engineered Plans and California Stock Plans are available for this home. Call 1-800-521-6797 for more information.

Design by
Home Planners,
Inc.

## Design Q3394

First Floor: 1,531 square feet
Second Floor: 1,307 square feet
Third Floor: 664 square feet
Total: 3,502 square feet

● Though somewhat less elaborate than other Victorian types, the Folk Victorian is nevertheless an important and delightful interpretation as evidenced by this three-story example. From lovely covered front porch to classic rear veranda, it offers the finest in modern floor plans. The formal living areas are set off by a family room which connects the main house to the service areas. The laundry has room for not only a washer and dryer but also a freezer and sewing area. The second floor holds three bedrooms and two full baths. A sitting area in the master suite separates it from family bedrooms. On the third floor is a guest bedroom with gracious bath and large walk-in closet. Note the large storage area in the third-floor hall.

Design by
Home Planners,
Inc.

## Design Q3388

First Floor: 1,517 square feet
Second Floor: 1,267 square feet
Third Floor: 480 square feet
Total: 3,264 square feet

Design by
Home Planners,
Inc.

● A testament to real Folk Victorian styling, this delightful home offers the best in thoughtful floor planning. From the covered front porch the home opens to a well-executed entry foyer. To the left is the casual family room with fireplace and proximity to the laundry and mud rooms. To the right is the formal living room with bay window and fireplace. This room connects to the formal dining area, also with bay window. The kitchen/breakfast room combination features sliding glass doors to the rear covered porch, an island cook top and large pantry. Second-floor bedrooms include a well-planned master suite and two family bedrooms served by a full bath. A guest room dominates the third floor and features its own private bath.

## Design Q9251

First Floor: 1,653 square feet
Second Floor: 700 square feet
Total: 2,353 square feet

● Beautiful arches and elaborate detail give the elevation of this four-bedroom, 1½-story home an unmistakable elegance. Inside the floor plan is equally appealing. Note the formal dining room with bay window, visible from the entrance hall. The large great room has a fireplace and a wall of windows out the back. A hearth room, with bookcase, adjoins the kitchen area with walk-in pantry. The master suite on the first floor features His and Hers wardrobes, a large whirlpool and double lavatories. Upstairs quarters share a full bath with compartmented sinks.

Design by
**Design Basics, Inc.**

# Design Q3386

First Floor: 1,683 square feet
Second Floor: 1,388 square feet
Third Floor: 808 square feet
Total: 3,879 square feet

● This beautiful Folk Victorian has all the properties of others in its class. Living areas include a formal Victorian parlor, a private study and large gathering room. The formal dining room has its more casual counterpart in a bay-windowed breakfast room. Both are near the well-appointed kitchen. Five bedrooms serve family and guest needs handily. Three bedrooms on the second floor include a luxurious master suite. For outdoor entertaining, there is a covered rear porch leading to a terrace.

Design by
Home Planners,
Inc.

## Design Q9269

First Floor: 1,081 square feet; Second Floor: 1,136 square feet
Total: 2,217 square feet

● Victorian charm and detailing radiate from the elevation of this four-bedroom, two-story design. Inside, formal living spaces, visible from the entry, begin with a dining room with hutch space and a parlor highlighted by a bayed window and alluring angles. the T-shaped staircase allows quick access to the informal spaces at the rear, such as the comfortable gathering room with a fireplace, built-in bookcase and many windows. Casual traffic patterns flow through a sunny, open breakfast area and island kitchen. Upstairs, a compartmented bath is shared by the secondary sleeping quarters. Gracing the master sleeping quarters is an elegant vaulted ceiling and private dressing/bath area offering an oval whirlpool, angled vanity and walk-in wardrobe.

Design by
Design
Basics,
Inc.

# CENTER-HALL COLONIAL FARMHOUSES

Colonial architecture is a reflection of a period of dedication to hard work, simple pleasures and solid virtues. As such, it brought together design characteristics that speak of symmetry and regularity of form. Straight lines and design details that were practical as well as ornamental took precedence over frivolous decoration. Floor plans featured square or rectangular rooms and stacked livability.

Popular today in the Northeastern region, particularly New England, the Center-Hall Colonial Farmhouse is an adaptation of the early homes built in the region and, as such, is a testament to symmetry and rigid adherence to traditional values. It is a classic, upright structure with a straight roof gable. The entry may be the only indication of ornamentation and can be detailed with a decorative frieze, pediment or portico over the front door. These details derive from Colonial and Georgian influences.

The characteristic central door opens to a center hall, from which all first-story rooms flow. This is usually where the stairwell to the second floor is found as well. These homes incorporate full two-story construction usually with all bedrooms found on the second floor.

Windows are regular, symmetrical and usually multi-paned and shuttered. Fireplace stacks are large, constructed of brick and may be placed centrally or to one end of the home. Horizontal wood siding is the most common exterior choice, but it is not unusual to see Center-Hall Colonials constructed in brick or part brick and part stone.

Garages and service areas tend to be appended to the main house with a service wing or entrance. In some cases, the connecting piece may be a family room or study.

Two fine examples of the Center-Hall Colonial Farmhouse are Design Q2188 and Design Q2610. Both have the symmetrical facade and straight-gabled roof that is common to Colonial architecture.

Design Q2188 features a strong center, brick chimney stack, a transommed double-door entry and a garage attached to the main house by a service entry. Added details include a weathervane at the end of the garage and symmetrical, shuttered windows.

Design Q2610 has two imposing brick chimneys and a front entry with transom and side lights. The garage on this plan attaches directly to the house and the windows remain unshuttered.

The fine grouping of Center-Hall Colonial Farmhouses offered in this section are apt reminders of America's architectural heritage. Large enough for virtually any family, they bring modern livability to a cherished historic style.

## Design Q2654

First Floor: 1,152 square feet
Second Floor: 844 square feet
Total: 1,996 square feet

● This is certainly an authentic traditional salt-box. It features a symmetrical design with a center fireplace, a wide, paneled doorway and multi-paned, double-hung windows. Tucked behind the one-car garage is a garden shed which provides work and storage space. The breakfast room features French doors which open onto a flagstone terrace. The U-shaped kitchen has built-in counters which make efficient use of space. The upstairs plan houses three bedrooms.

Design by
Home Planners,
Inc.

Design by
**Home Planners,
Inc.**

# Design Q2188

First Floor: 1,440 square feet
Second Floor: 1,280 square feet
Total: 2,720 square feet

● This design is characteristic of early America and its presence will create an atmosphere of that time in our heritage. However, it will be right at home wherever located. Along with exterior charm, this design has outstanding livability to offer its occupants. Beginning with the first floor, there are formal and informal areas plus the work centers. Note the center bath which has direct access from three adjacent areas. Built-in book shelves are the feature of both the family room and the study/bedroom. Built-ins are also featured in the garage. Ascending up to the second floor, one will be in the private sleeping area. This area consists of the master suite, three bedrooms and full bath. Folding stairs are in the upstairs hall for easy access to the attic.

## Design Q9300

First Floor: 1,137 square feet
Second Floor: 917 square feet
Total: 2,054 square feet

● Colonial detailing and gracious amenities makes this home ideal for a variety of lifestyles. A bright dining room opens to a hard-surfaced entry. Access the private den with bookcase via French doors. Family gatherings are comfortable in the great room with fireplace, built-in bookcase and large bayed windows at the rear. An island kitchen benefits from a pantry, desk and sunny breakfast area with outdoor access. The upstairs landing is brightened by a skylight. In the master bedroom there is a vaulted ceiling, plus a dressing area featuring a walk-in closet with mirrored bi-pass doors and window seat. Secondary bedrooms share a hall bath with window seat while the front bedroom has its own window seat. Truly, this is a delightful home inside and out!

Design by
Design
Basics,
Inc.

## Design Q9301

First Floor: 1,279 square feet
Second Floor: 1,241 square feet
Total: 2,520 square feet

● Colonial flavor is evident on the elevation of this four-bedroom, two-story home. A separate service entry with a closet directly accesses the laundry/mud room. Entertaining will be enjoyable in the formal dining and living rooms. In the large family room, there is a beautiful segmented arched transom window and fireplace. Nearby is the island kitchen with snack bar, built-in desk, two generous pantries and sunny dinette. On the second level, two front secondary bedrooms feature window seats. Adjacent to a third secondary bedroom is an unfinished storage area. Two lavs grace the large hall bath. A vaulted master bedroom with His and Hers closets has double doors leading into a dressing room. This area contains a large whirlpool and two lavs. At 2,520 square feet, many family-style amenities are designed into this home.

Design by
Design
Basics,
Inc.

## Design Q2657

First Floor: 1,217 square feet
Second Floor: 868 square feet
Total: 2,085 square feet

Design by
Home Planners,
Inc.

● Deriving its design from the traditional Cape Cod style, this facade features clapboard siding, small-paned windows and a transom-lit entrance flanked by carriage lamps. A central chimney services two fireplaces, one in the country-kitchen and the other in the formal living room which is removed from the disturbing flow of traffic. The master suite is located to the left of the upstairs landing. A full bathroom services two additional bedrooms on the second floor.

## Design Q1701

First Floor: 1,344 square feet
Second Floor: 948 square feet
Total: 2,292 square feet

● The garage wing of this Cape closely resembles the main dwelling: narrow clapboards, shutters and lintels over the multi-paned windows all match exactly. A narrow, shaded porch leads into the family room, which has twin bookcases framing the raised hearth as well as a rustic beamed ceiling. The study downstairs easily converts to a guest bedroom and is conveniently served by a bath that boasts its own shower. This bath opens to the back hall so that it can be reached easily from the back rooms in the house. Two of the upstairs bedrooms have both dressing rooms and walk-in closets. The secondary bedrooms can, like the master bedroom, be opened up into one commodious room by removing the wall in between them.

Design by
Home Planners,
Inc.

## Design Q3505

First Floor: 2,899 square feet
Second Floor: 1,519 square feet
Total: 4,418 square feet

● A sweeping veranda with tapered columns supports the low-pitched roof and its delicately detailed cornice work. The wood railing effectively complements the lattice-work below. Horizontal siding and double-hung windows with muntins and shutters enhance the historic appeal of this 1½-story home. Inside, the spacious central foyer has a high ceiling and a dramatic, curving staircase to the second floor. Two formal areas flank the foyer and include the living room to the left and the dining room to the right. The U-shaped kitchen easily services the latter through a butler's pantry. A library and gathering room flank the kitchen and will delight the family. Sleeping accommodations excel with a spacious master suite. Here, a private bath and two closets—one a walk-in—guarantee satisfaction. At the top of the dramatic staircase to the second floor is a generous sitting area which looks down on the foyer. Three bedrooms are directly accessible from this area. A bonus room further enhances this fabulous family home.

Design by
Home Planners,
Inc.

## Design Q3566

First Floor: 1,635 square feet
Second Floor: 586 square feet
Total: 2,221 square feet
Bonus Room: 321 square feet

● Don't be fooled by the humble appearance of this farmhouse. All the amenities abound. Covered porches are located to both the front and rear of the home. A grand front entrance opens into living and dining rooms. The family will surely enjoy the ambience of the keeping room with its fireplace and beamed ceiling. A service entry, with laundry nearby, separates the garage from the main house. An over-the-garage bonus room allows for room to grow or a nice study. Two quaint bedrooms and full bath make up the second floor. Each bedroom features a lovely dormer window.

Design by
Home Planners,
Inc.

## Design Q1956
First Floor: 990 square feet
Second Floor: 728 square feet; Total: 1,718 square feet

Design by
Home Planners,
Inc.

Three-Bedroom Option

● Simple, functional, and loaded with Colonial appeal, this versatile two-story plan features the finest in family floor plans. To the right of the entry foyer, a large formal living area connects to the dining room, allowing adequate space for entertaining in style. The U-shaped kitchen features a pass-through counter to the breakfast room. The sunken family room is enhanced by a beamed ceiling, raised-hearth fireplace, and built-in bookshelves. Upstairs are four bedrooms (or choose the three-bedroom option included in the blueprint package). Other highlights of the plan include a full-length rear terrace and storage space galore. For information on customizing this design, call 1-800-521-6797, ext. 800.

## Design Q2540

First Floor: 1,306 square feet
Second Floor: 1,360 square feet
Total: 2,666 square feet

● This comfortable Colonial home puts a good foot forward in family living. The entry hall is wide and gracious to receive guests (and comes complete with a powder room for convenience). Flanking it are the family room with fireplace and the formal living room. A dining room has sliding glass doors to a rear terrace and leads directly to the L-shaped kitchen with island range. A handy utility area features washer/dryer space and storage and has an exterior door to the two-car garage. Upstairs are four bedrooms with two full baths. The master bedroom has a sitting room, dressing area, walk-in closet and bath with dual vanities.

Design by
Home Planners,
Inc.

## Design Q9239

First Floor: 998 square feet
Second Floor: 1,206 square feet
Total: 2,204 square feet

● The bright entry of this two-story home opens to formal living and dining space. To the back is the more informal family room with fireplace and built-in bookshelves. An island kitchen features a corner sink, pantry and convenient planning desk. Upstairs, the master bedroom has a vaulted ceiling and sumptuous master bath with skylit dressing area, whirlpool tub, and walk-in closet. Three family bedrooms and a full bath round out sleeping accommodations. Note the laundry area on the second floor as well.

Design by
**Design Basics, Inc.**

## Design Q2659 First Floor: 1,023 square feet
Second Floor: 1,008 square feet; Third Floor: 476 square feet
Total: 2,507 square feet

● The facade of this three-storied, pitch-roofed house has a symmetrical placement of windows and a restrained but elegant central entrance. The central hall, or foyer, expands midway through the house to a family kitchen. Off the foyer are two rooms, a living room with fireplace and a study. The windowed third floor attic can be used as a study and studio. Three bedrooms are housed on the second floor.

Design by
Home Planners,
Inc.

## Design Q2322

First Floor: 1,480 square feet
Second Floor: 1,172 square feet
Total: 2,652 square feet

Design by
**Home Planners,
Inc.**

● Angular in configuration, this home offers loads of livability. There are five bedrooms on the second floor as well as two full baths. The first floor has a 27-foot living room with fireplace and a formal dining room with bay window. The U-shaped kitchen features eating space and is located nearby the informal family room with beamed ceiling. For quiet times, there is a study off the front foyer. The garage is angled and features a quaint covered porch. It has a large storage area plus smaller closet for holding all the necessities.

## Design Q2610

First Floor: 1,505 square feet
Second Floor: 1,344 square feet
Total: 2,849 square feet

Design by
Home Planners,
Inc.

● This full two-story traditional will be worthy of note
wherever built. It strongly recalls images of a New England of yesteryear. And well it might; for the window
treatment is delightful. The front entrance detail is
inviting. The narrow horizontal siding and the corner
boards are appealing as are the two massive chimneys.
The center entrance hall is large with a handy powder
room nearby. The study has built-in bookshelves and
offers a full measure of privacy. The interior kitchen has
a pass-through to the family room and enjoys all that natural light from the bay window of the nook. A beamed
ceiling, fireplace and sliding glass doors are features of
the family room. The mud room highlights a closet, laundry equipment and an extra wash room. Study the upstairs with those four bedrooms, two baths and plenty of
closets. An excellent arrangement for all.

## Design Q9303

First Floor: 1,428 square feet
Second Floor: 1,304 square feet
Total: 2,732 square feet

● Nine-foot main level walls are a nice feature not readily apparent in the design of this popular Colonial home. Comfortable traffic patterns segregate formal and informal living spaces. To the left of the spacious two-story entry is a formal dining room with hutch space. Sunny windows bring light into the living room and throughout the whole home. The built-in bookcases in a generous family room can easily be

converted to a wet bar. Highlights of the island kitchen/breakfast area are a wraparound counter, planning desk, walk-in pantry and a butler pantry. Upstairs, secondary bedrooms are served by a compartmented hall bath with double lavs. The large master suite sports a vaulted ceiling, His and Hers closets, corner whirlpool and double vanity with makeup counter

Design by
**Design Basics, Inc.**

© 1989 design basics inc.

## Design Q9302

First Floor: 1,536 square feet
Second Floor: 1,343 square feet
Total: 2,879 square feet

● A delightful elevation will be appreciated by anyone aspiring to live in Colonial comfort. Three arches encompass the covered porch at the service entry to mud/laundry room. Inside, bright windows shed sunlight into the formal dining room with serving buffet. To the right of the elegant two-story entry is the living room. Sparkling French doors access the private den with bookcases from the spacious great room. In the roomy island kitchen, cooks will enjoy the built-in pantry and breakfast area. Be sure to notice the fireplace in the spacious master suite with three closets and a built-in dresser. A sophisticated skylit master bath has a two-person whirlpool and plant shelf. The compartmented bath upstairs has a separate tub and shower for the secondary bedrooms.

Design by
Design
Basics,
Inc.

## Design Q2687 First Floor: 1,819 square feet
Second Floor: 1,431 square feet; Total: 3,250 square feet

● Exterior styling of this home is reminiscent of the past but its floor plan is as up-to-date as it can get. Its many unique features include: a greenhouse, 78 square feet, off the country kitchen, a media room for all the modern electronic equipment, a hobby/laundry room with a washroom and a deluxe master bath.

Design by
**Home Planners,
Inc.**

Design by
Home Planners,
Inc.

## Design Q2731

First Floor: 1,039 square feet
Second Floor: 973 square feet
Total: 2,012 square feet

● Affordable style is the hallmark of this Colonial design. The U-shaped kitchen with large pantry and adjacent breakfast nook is a big center of attention. Next to it is a formal dining room. Living room with fireplace, first-floor study, and efficient service area round out a hardworking downstairs plan. The second floor features a sizable master suite, complete with twin vanities and roomy walk-in closet.

## Design Q2998

First Floor: 2,243 square feet
Second Floor: 1,532 square feet
Total: 3,775 square feet

● Symmetrical and simply lovely, this gambrel-roofed two-story is a fine example of historical homes. Its details will enchant the most particular enthusiast of early architecture. The floor plan is a classic as well. Note the formal dining and living rooms flanking the entry hall. The living room has a fireplace and the dining room a bay window. A media room/study also sports a fireplace and has access to a rear terrace. The family room connects to the kitchen via a through snack bar. There's also another fireplace here. On the second floor are three bedrooms and two full baths. The third floor contains unfinished space which acts as superb storage and can be developed later into more bedrooms if needed.

Design by
Home Planners,
Inc.

## Design Q2538

First Floor: 1,503 square feet
Second Floor: 1,095 square feet
Total: 2,598 square feet

● This SaltBox is charming, indeed. The livability it has to offer to the large and growing family is great. The entry is spacious and is open to the second floor balcony. For living areas, there is the study in addition to the living and family rooms. The large kitchen has an island range and attached nook with sliding glass doors to the terrace. The master suite, on the second floor, has its own fireplace and a large walk-in closet in the dressing area. Three more bedrooms share a full bath.

Design by
Home Planners,
Inc.

Design by
**Design
Basics,
Inc.**

TRAPS

OPEN TO
BELOW

DISPLAY

**Br. 2**
13⁰x12³

BOOKS

LIN.

LIN.

**Br. 3**
12⁰x13⁰

OPEN TO
BELOW

DN

**Br. 4**
12⁰x13⁰

TRAPS

8'-8"
CLG.

**Bfst.**
15⁰x11⁴

**Den**
11⁸x13⁴

**Kit.**
13⁰x10⁹

DESK

**Grt. rm.**
16⁰x20⁸

W/P

WET BAR

12'-0"
CEILING

CATHEDRAL
CEILING

UP    DN

51'-4"

**Gar.**
20⁸x31⁴

**Din.**
12⁰x14⁰

**E.**

**Liv.**
12⁰x15⁰

**Mbr.**
13⁰x16³

10'-0" CEILING

CVRD.
STOOP

72'-8"

© 1990 design basics inc.

## Design Q9299

First Floor: 2,063 square feet
Second Floor: 894 square feet
Total: 2,957 square feet

● An elegant brick elevation and rows
of shuttered windows lend timeless
beauty to this 1½-story Colonial design.
The volume entry surveys formal dining and living rooms and the magnificent great room. Sparkling floor-to-ceil-
ing windows flank the fireplace in the
great room with a cathedral ceiling.
French doors, bayed windows and a
decorative ceiling, plus a wet bar highlight the private den. Special lifestyle
amenities in the kitchen and bayed
breakfast area include a built-in desk,
wrapping counters and island. A boxed
ceiling adds elegance to the master
suite. In the master bath/dressing area,
note the large walk-in closet, built-in
dresser, His and Hers vanities, oval
whirlpool and plant shelves. Each secondary bedroom upstairs has a roomy
closet and private bath.

# EUROPEAN-INSPIRED FARMHOUSES

Centuries before coming to the New World, Europeans enjoyed farmhouse styles that were uniquely their own. Built originally of simple materials, these dwellings were functional, cozy and sturdy. They also reflected the distinct design bent of the country in which they were found, particularly with regard to rooflines. French country houses had the classic hipped roof so favored in that region; the Dutch maintained gambrel roofs; and the English added gabled roofs (often thatched) to their cottages. Each group incorporated design details that blended to charming result in the European-Inspired Farmhouse.

These homes are a development of European styles and influences imposed on basic American farmhouse structure. They represent an adaptation of those homes found in the countrysides of France, Germany, Holland and other Western European nations.

In general, the European Farmhouse has a classic, upright two-story stature. Like their historic equivalents, these homes may be characterized most easily by their roof types. While most are straight and gabled, they may vary to hipped versions in the French style or gambreled (or double-pitched) in the Flemish and Dutch tradition.

The windows, as well, echo European styling. Special details include metal-clad French bows and dormers, Dutch dormers protruding from the roof, Greek stone or brick arches over windows and doors, and the classic Palladian-style window grouping.

Siding on these homes is almost exclusively wood but may be accented with brick, stone or even stucco.

Among the European-Inspired Farmhouses in this section are some outstanding examples of the influences of various countries on the architectural details of the homes. Design Q9857, for instance, has many of the features of Country French homes: French bows with metal-clad roofs, a Palladian window and additional shuttered windows. Design Q9306 exudes more of a Modern French style with a strongly hipped roof and narrow, transommed windows. Dutch and Flemish design is apparent in Design Q2697 and Design Q9860. Both have gambrel roofs and twin chimney stacks, but Q9860 is sided almost entirely in stone while Q2697 sports only a stone fireplace.

All of the representative homes are alive with European country charm in conjunction with the best in up-to-date floor planning.

Copyright 1992 Stephen S. Fuller, Inc.

## Design Q9870

First Floor: 2,155 square feet
Second Floor: 1,020 square feet
Total: 3,175 square feet

● To highlight the exterior of this home, wood siding and paneled shutters have been artfully combined with arched transoms, gables and a sweeping roof line to define the beautiful glass entry. The open foyer at once reveals the large living and dining rooms and a classic great room with coffered ceiling and hearth. Double doors open to the master bedroom with unique tray ceiling and fireplace. The master bath includes knee space with double vanities and shower, corner garden tub and His and Hers closets. The exercise room can be accessed from either the master bedroom or great room and opens onto the porch at the rear of the home. The generous corner breakfast area also opens to the porch. The large kitchen with a cook-top island, pantry and laundry room complete the main level. The gallery features built-in bookshelves and computer/study nook with easy access from all three bedrooms on the upper level. An unfinished bonus room with attic access offers room for expansion.

Design by
**Design Traditions
Atlanta**

WIDTH 62'
DEPTH 63'

# Design Q9869

First Floor: 1,475 square feet
Second Floor: 1,460 square feet
Total: 2,935 square feet

● This English country home of stucco and stone features elliptical keystone detailing and a covered entranceway. Through the columned entry, the two-story foyer opens to the living room with wet bar. The media room features a fireplace and is accessed from both the main hall and great room. A hall powder room and coat closet are located to the rear of the foyer. The two-story great room with fireplace is open to the breakfast area, kitchen and rear staircase, making entertaining a pleasure. The kitchen design is ideal with breakfast bar and preparation island and is conveniently located near the laundry room. The dining room with its elliptical window is ideal for formal entertaining. The upper level begins with the balcony landing overlooking the great room. The master bedroom features a bay-windowed sitting area and a tray ceiling. The master bath has dual vanities, a corner garden tub, separate shower, a large walk-in closet and an optional secret room. Across the balcony, Bedrooms 2 and 3 share a bath. Bedroom 4 in the front of the home has a private bath.

Design by
**Design Traditions**
**Atlanta**

Width 57'-6"
Depth 46'-6"

Copyright 1992 Stephen S. Fuller, Inc.

## Design Q9855

Square footage: 2,902

● A one-story plan for even a large family, this home provides all the necessities and many luxuries as well. For formal occasions, there's a grand dining room just off the entry foyer. It has a vaulted ceiling and is just across the hall from the gourmet kitchen. The great room has beautiful ceiling treatment and access to the rear deck. For more casual times, the breakfast nook and adjoining keeping room with fireplace fill the bill. The master suite is huge and contains every amenity. Its sitting room allows access to the rear deck. Note the gigantic walk-in closet here. Two family bedrooms share a full bath. Each of these bedrooms has its own lavatory.

Design by
**Design Traditions**
Atlanta

Width 71'
Depth 66'

Copyright 1992 Stephen S. Fuller, Inc.

## Design Q9856 First Floor: 1,450 square feet
Second Floor: 1,500 square feet; Total: 2,950 square feet

● A gambrel roof, stone and wood frame exterior, flower boxes and accent shutters create this Dutch country cottage. Round accent windows frame the arched entrance with keystone details and double entrance doors. The spacious two-story foyer and staircase are interestingly designed with a landing to the right of the foyer and powder room to the left. The family room with wet bar, bay-windowed breakfast area and kitchen are open to one another, creating a practical living space that converts easily for entertaining. The laundry room is located between the kitchen and the two-car garage, with an additional door to the back yard. The dining room has an attractive bay window at one end and an opening to the living room on the other. The upper level begins with a landing overlooking the open foyer. Passing through double doors to the master bedroom, a tray ceiling and a luxurious sitting room with deep bay window are showcased. Diagonally set double doors lead to the master bath with a corner garden tub, two vanities and separate shower. Three bedrooms and two full baths complete the upper level.

Design by
**Design Traditions**
Atlanta

Width 57'-8"
Depth 42'-4"

Copyright 1992 Stephen S. Fuller, Inc.

## Design Q9857

First Floor: 1,156 square feet
Second Floor: 1,239 square feet
Total: 2,395 square feet

● This Traditional home combines an attractive classic exterior with an open and sophisticated interior design. On approach, notice the use of brick and siding, Palladian and box bay windows, flower boxes and a covered entrance flanked by columns. The two-story foyer has a staircase to the left and a coat closet and powder room straight ahead. Proceeding right from the foyer are both the living and dining rooms with their individual window treatments. Entering the kitchen from the dining room is a corner butler pantry for added convenience while entertaining. The open design flows from the breakfast area to the family room with two large bay windows. The open foyer staircase leads to the upper level, beginning with the master suite. The bay window extends the eye beyond the attractive master bedroom. The master bath contains a luxurious tub, separate shower and dual vanities, as well as a large linen closet. A large walk-in master closet completes the suite. Bedroom 2 is inviting with its bay window and large closet. All three secondary bedrooms share a hall bath with separate vanity and bathing areas.

Design by
### Design Traditions
Atlanta

Width 54'
Depth 39'-5"

Copyright 1992 Stephen S Fuller

# Design Q9858 First Floor: 1,570 square feet
Second Floor: 1,630 square feet; Total: 3,200 square feet

● This classic Americana design employs wood siding, a variety of window styles, and a detailed front porch. Upon entry, the large two-story foyer flows into the formal dining room with arched window accents and the combination study and living room with a large bay window. A short passage with wet bar accesses the family room with a wall of windows, French doors and a fireplace. The large breakfast area and open kitchen with cooking island are spacious and airy as well as efficient. The walk-in pantry, laundry, and entry to the two-car garage complete this level. Upstairs, the master suite's sleeping and sitting room feature architectural details including columns, tray ceilings and a fireplace. The elegant master bath contains a raised oval tub, dual vanities and separate shower. Generous His and Hers closets are located beyond the bath. Additional bedrooms are complete with closets and a variety of bath combinations.

Design by
**Design Traditions**
Atlanta

Width 59'-10"
Depth 43'-4"

## Design Q3442

Square Footage: 1,273

● For those just starting out or the empty-nester, this unique one-story plan is sure to delight. A covered porch introduces a dining room with coffered ceiling and views out two sides of the house. The kitchen is just off this room and is most efficient with a double sink, dishwasher and pantry. The living room gains attention with a volume ceiling, fireplace, and access to a covered patio. The master bedroom also features a volume ceiling while enjoying the luxury of a private bath. In it, a washer/dryer, walk-in closet, double-bowl vanity, garden tub, separate shower and compartmented toilet comprise the amenities. Not to be overlooked, a second bedroom may easily convert to a media room or study—the choice is yours. For information on customizing this design, call 1-800-521-6797, ext. 800.

Design by
Home Planners, Inc.

## Design Q2655

First Floor: 893 square feet
Second Floor: 652 square feet
Total: 1,545 square feet

Design by
Home Planners,
Inc.

● Wonderful things can be enclosed in small packages. This is the case for this two-story design. The total square footage is a mere 1,545 square feet yet its features are many, indeed. Its exterior appeal is very eye-pleasing with horizontal lines and two second story dormers. Livability will be enjoyed in this plan. The front study is ideal for a quiet escape. Nearby is a powder room also convenient to the kitchen and breakfast room. Two bedrooms and two full baths are located on the second floor.

## Design Q3481A

Square Footage: 1,901

● In just under 2,000 square feet, this pleasing one-story home bears all the livability of houses twice its size. A combined living and dining room offers elegance for entertaining; with two elevations to choose from, the living room can either support an octagonal bay or a bumped-out nook. The U-shaped kitchen finds easy access to the breakfast nook and rear family room; sliding glass doors lead from the family room to a back stoop. The master bedroom has a quaint potshelf and a private bath with a spa tub, a double-bowl vanity, a walk-in closet and a compartmented toilet. With two additional family bedrooms—one may serve as a den if desired—and a hall bath with dual lavatories, this plan offers the best in accommodations. Both elevations come with the blueprint package. For information on customizing this design, call 1-800-521-6797, ext. 800.

### Design Q3481B

Square Footage: 1,908

WIDTH 42'
DEPTH 63'-6"

Design by
Home Planners,
Inc.

# Design Q3460

Square Footage: 1,389

● A double dose of charm, this special farmhouse plan offers two elevations in its blueprint package—one showcases a delightful wraparound porch. Though rooflines and porch options are different, the floor plan is basically the same and very livable. A formal living room has a warming fireplace and a delightful bay window. The kitchen separates this area from the more casual family room. In the kitchen, you'll find an efficient snack bar that services the family room, as well as a pantry for additional storage space. Three bedrooms include two family bedrooms served by a full bath and a lovely master suite with its own private bath with separate lavatories. Notice the location of the washer and dryer—convenient to all of the bedrooms. For information on customizing this design, call 1-800-521-6797, xt. 800.

Design by
Home Planners,
Inc.

## Design Q3507

First Floor: 1,360 square feet
Second Floor: 1,172 square feet
Total: 2,532 square feet

● After a brisk walk to the creek for some fly fishing or an invigorating day of raking leaves, enjoy some spiced hot apple cider by one of the four fireplaces highlighted in this delightful farmhouse. Leading inside is an elevated front entrance with a dual set of steps, an appealing patterned railing and a muntined door flanked by carriage lamps, all of which projects an engaging image of the raised

cottage so popular in the South. To the left of the foyer is the formal living room with a corner fireplace. To the right is a formal dining room which also enjoys a fireplace. Open planning is the byword of the spacious family living area. An efficient kitchen possesses a cooking island, a snack bar, a planning desk and a breakfast area with access to the veranda. Twin pillars support an archway opening to the large family room which is enhanced by yet another fireplace. The expansive master bedroom is complemented by a sitting area and a warming fireplace. A luxurious master bath offers a vanity flanked by twin lavatories, a whirlpool bath, a shower and a large walk-in closet.

WIDTH 44'
DEPTH 42'

Design by
Home Planners,
Inc.

## Design Q2689 First Floor: 1,385 square feet
Second Floor: 982 square feet; Total: 2,367 square feet

● This cozy three-bedroom Gambrel offers charming elegance with country comfort. A large country kitchen with bay overlooks a rear terrace. There's also a separate dining room downstairs, plus a living room and screened porch. All three bedrooms are upstairs, away from the distractions of rest of the house.

Design by
Home Planners, Inc.

## Design Q9305

Square Footage: 2,015

● Romantic appeal radiates from the elegant covered porch and gracious features of this ranch home. A formal dining room with bright windows is viewed from the entry. In the great room, featuring an entertainment center and bookcases, warmth emanates from the three-sided through-fireplace. Homeowners will enjoy the cozy retreat of the bay-windowed hearth room with 10-foot ceiling. Near the hearth is an open breakfast area and kitchen with snack bar, pantry and ample counter space. A window seat framed by closets highlights secondary Bedroom 2. The third bedroom easily converts to an optional den for quiet study. Designed for privacy, the master suite enjoys a boxed ceiling, skylit dressing area with His and Hers lavs, corner whirlpool and large walk-in closet. With many dramatic elements, this will be the home of your dreams!

Design by
**Design Basics, Inc.**

## Design Q9304
Square Footage: 1,850

● European style influences the elevation of this distinctive ranch home. Appealing rooflines and a covered porch with repeating arches provide stunning curb appeal. Inside, an impressive 10-foot high entry greets family and friends. An open concept pervades the kitchen/dinette area. Picture your family enjoying the bayed eating area, wrapping counters, desk, island and wet/bar servery ideal for entertaining. The decorative hutch space adds appeal to a formal dining room. Bright windows frame a fireplace in the great room. Sure to please is the service entry to the laundry/mud room with soaking sink and counter space. Bedroom 2 can easily be converted into a private den. A boxed ceiling decorates the master suite while three windows provide natural lighting. Dual lavs, a walk-in closet, whirlpool and cedar-lined window seat enhance the master bath.

Design by
Design
Basics,
Inc.

## Design Q9306

First Floor: 1,268 square feet
Second Floor: 1,075 square feet
Total: 2,343 square feet

● Captivating! A covered front porch hints at the comfort within. An added perk is the large 3-car garage. Formal rooms are surveyed by the entry. To the right, a volume ceiling, elegant windows and through-fireplace lend atmosphere to the living room. A volume family room includes repeating arched windows, an entertainment center and bookcases. The sunny dinette area is served by a roomy kitchen with wrapping counters, snack bar and planning desk. Convenience was designed into the main floor utility/laundry room and large closet. Upstairs, comfortable secondary bedrooms are served by a walk-in linen closet and bath with dual lavs. French doors lead into the master suite with vaulted ceiling, whirlpool, dual vanities and a huge walk-in closet.

Design by
Design
Basics,
Inc.

© design basics inc. 1991

# Design Q9267

Square Footage: 2,068

● Walk through an elegant
covered veranda to enter this
spacious ranch home. A spectacular window provides a
view out the back from the
expansive great room.
Gathering areas are warmed
by a three-sided fireplace and
served by a well-planned
kitchen with a pantry, desk
and island counter with snack
bar. An irresistible master
suite features a private covered deck and a pampering
dressing area with a whirlpool
and large walk-in closet. The
den could be used as a third
bedroom with an alternate
door location. An abundance
of windows throughout the
plan brightens this home.

COVERED DECK

Hrth.
10⁸ x 10⁴

Bfst.
12⁸ x 11¹⁰
8'-8" CLG.

Grt. rm.
15⁰ x 20⁰
10'-8" CEILING

SNACK BAR

Kit.
12⁸ x 11⁴

Mbr.
15⁰ x 13⁴
9'-0" CLG.

GLASS BLOCK

W/P

LIN.

DRESSER

Br. 2
11⁰ x 11⁰

LIN.

Den
11³ x 14²
10'-0" CEILING
OPT. BEDROOM

DN
UP

Din.
11⁴ x 14⁰
10'-0" CLG.

STORAGE

W. D.

Gar.
22⁰ x 21⁴

COVERED VERANDA

56'-0"

66'-0"

© 1990 design basics inc.

Design by
Design
Basics,
Inc.

133

## Design Q2697

First Floor: 1,752 square feet
Second Floor: 1,486 square feet
Total: 3,238 square feet

Design by
**Home Planners,
Inc.**

● This two-story design with gambrel roof is reminiscent of the histori
home of Robert Nicolson, Williamsburg tailor and merchant. He built
his house around 1751. Our updated floor plan includes a large rear
family room with raised-hearth fireplace and a large front living room
with fireplace. A convenience kitchen offers pass-through to an inform
eating area off the family room. The house includes a formal dining
room as well. Upstairs are four bedrooms, including a master suite.

## Design Q2680 First Floor: 1,707 square feet
Second Floor: 1,439 square feet; Total: 3,146 square feet

Design by
Home Planners,
Inc.

● This Early American, Dutch Colonial not only has charm, but offers many fine features. The foyer allows easy access to all rooms on the first floor - excellent livability. Note the large country kitchen with beamed ceiling, fireplace and island cook top. A large, formal dining room and powder room are only a few steps away. A fireplace also will be found in the study and living room. The service area, mud room, wash room and laundry are tucked near the garage. Two bedrooms, full bath and master bedroom suite will be found on the second floor. A fourth bedroom and bath are accessible through the master bedroom or stairs in the service entrance.

Copyright 1992 Stephen S. Fuller, Inc.

# Design Q9859

First Floor: 1,333 square feet
Second Floor: 1,425 square feet
Total: 2,758 square feet

● This Early American design possesses a rare charm, largely due to its proportions and breezeway. True to tradition are the gambrel roof, brick and siding combination, covered entrance and detailed columns and balustrade. The main level begins with equally proportioned dining and living rooms framed by columns. A powder room is located on the right before the great room complete with fireplace and a wall of windows. The kitchen is large and opens directly onto the breezeway porch, which leads to the two-car garage. The upper level begins with a children's den at the top of the staircase. Just beyond, the private guest bedroom awaits visitors with a complete bath and walk-in closet. Additional bedrooms feature a shared bath, generous closets and dormer windows. The master suite consists of a very large sleeping area with fireplace, a master bath with bay window, separate shower and two walk-in closets.

Width 69'-2"
Depth 46'-10"

Design by
**Design Traditions**
Atlanta

# Design Q9860

First Floor: 1,530 square feet
Second Floor: 1,515 square feet
Total: 3,045 square feet

Design by
**Design Traditions**
Atlanta

● The Country French charm of this home is irresistible; with gambrel roof, combined use of stone and wood, and segmented stone arch window detailing. The two-story foyer with staircase and tray ceiling gives a first impression of space and style. The large living and dining rooms are complemented by large window areas, a fireplace and detailed columns. The art of cooking is emphasized in the kitchen, with a work island and charming breakfast room that opens into a large family room with fireplace and wet bar. A second staircase from the family room allows easy access to the upper level. Touring the upper level, the hallway leads to additional bedrooms, both with large closets and a shared bath. A fourth bedroom has a walk-in closet and private bath. The master suite includes a large bay-windowed sitting area, a luxurious master bath and an extensive walk-in closet, as well as a perfectly located exercise room or hideaway.

## Design Q3497

First Floor: 1,581 square feet
Second Floor: 592 square feet
Total: 2,173 square feet

● This handsome bungalow would make a perfect first home for new families. Picture a hanging swing on the front porch and a self-contained play or leisure area on the back porch just off the family room. The large kitchen and breakfast area allows Mom to cook without kids under foot and the master bedroom maintains privacy due to its positioning behind the master bath. The two upstairs bedrooms also provide lots of room and privacy. The living room, just off the foyer, presents an ideal place for families to gather in the evenings around the cozy fireplace.

Design by
**Home Planners, Inc.**

# COUNTRY-STYLE CAPES & COTTAGES

Country Capes and Cottages are simple, economical homes with a New England Colonial heritage. They have roots in the down-to-earth shelters constructed by the early settlers which featured a basic, boxy design. These early models were small, square and simple, and, consequently, were easy to construct. They provided practical housing that could be expanded as needed. Today's Country Cape fits comfortably almost anywhere but works especially well situated on the smaller lots in lakeside and seaside settings.

The modern versions of this style are constructed in simple box-like fashion usually with classic horizontal siding and a steeply pitched gabled roof. They may be a full Cape with a center-hall floor plan or the entry may be off-center as in the half-Cape or the three-quarter Cape. Many are designed to "grow" by the addition of winged appendages that give these great starter houses an expandable nature.

Following classic traditional architecture for a facade, the Country Cape may be updated nicely with projecting dormers and sun rooms to the rear. They almost always feature symmetric, multi-paned shuttered windows and may include dormers on the second floor.

Decorative detailing may be very sparse or can include dove-cotes, cupolas, and arched garage doors or service entries. Some versions even have Victorian-style gingerbread details. Western examples of the Country Cape are more rustic and cabin-like and often include a front porch. It is common to see this style used for second homes or leisure living because of their time-honored design and low building costs.

Country Capes seem almost to be defined by their expandable nature. Consider, for example, Design Q2682 in this section which begins as a simple "half house" then adds double wings for a study and a garage. A large plan, Design Q2699, is a Full Telescoping Cape with multiple wings and true Cape Cod, 1½-story style.

Adapted versions include Design Q2615, a Modified Country Cape, and Design Q9007, a Victorian-Style Cape. Though both of these designs have elements of Cape Cod design, they have been altered with details borrowed from other styles to create a new look. Likewise, Designs Q2661 and Q9666 have taken on more dramatic country elements: shake roof, covered front porch, stone chimney stack.

Always a favorite, Cape Cods gain even more popularity when done in country accents. This section of Country-Style Capes and Cottages shows off the best components of this adapted design.

## Design Q2682

First Floor (Basic Plan): 976 square feet
First Floor (Expanded Plan): 1,230 square feet
Second Floor (Both Plans): 744 square feet
Total (Basic Plan): 1,720 square feet
Total (Expanded Plan): 1,974 square feet

● Here is an expandable Colonial with a full measure of Cape Cod Charm. For those who wish to build the basic house, there is an abundance of low-budget livability. Twin fireplaces serve the formal living room and the informal country kitchen. Note the spaciousness of both areas. A dining room and powder room are also on the first floor of this basic plan. Upstairs three bedrooms and two full baths.

Design by
Home Planners, Inc.

**60'-0"**

TERRACE

COVERED PORCH

DINING RM.
10⁸ x 12⁰

COUNTRY KITCHEN
20⁰ x 13⁰ - 15⁸

GARAGE
13⁸ x 20⁴

STUDY
13⁶ x 18⁰

PDR. RM.

FOYER

BOOKS

LIVING RM.
20⁰ x 13⁰

PORCH

**35'-0"**

ROOF

BEDROOM
12¹⁰ x 9⁸

BEDROOM
12¹⁰ x 9⁸

ATTIC STORAGE
(FUTURE ROOM)

ROOF

LINEN

DN

BATH

BATH

MASTER BEDROOM
11¹⁰ x 14⁰

ROOF

ROOF

● This expanded version of the basic house on the opposite page is equally as reminiscent of Cape Cod. Common in the 17th-Century was the addition of appendages to the main structure. This occurred as family size increased or finances improved. This version provides for the addition of wings to accommodate a large study and a garage. Utilizing the alcove behind the study results in a big, covered porch. Certainly a charming design whichever version you decide to build for your family.

## Design Q2571

First Floor: 1,137 square feet
Second Floor: 795 square feet
Total: 1,932 square feet

● This cozy Cape has an efficient plan that's long on affordable livability. Note the comfortable family room, which has both a fireplace and snack bar; separate dining room with gorgeous bay window; formal living room; and full bath down next to a study that could also be a fourth bedroom. Upstairs are three bedrooms, including a master suite, and two more full bathrooms.

Design by
Home Planners,
Inc.

## Design Q2852 First Floor: 919 square feet
Second Floor: 535 square feet; Total: 1,454 square feet

● Compact enough for even the smallest lot, this cozy design provides comfortable living space for a small family. At the heart of the plan is a spacious country kitchen. It features a cooking island, snack bar, and a dining area that opens to a house-wide rear terrace. The nearby dining room also opens to the terrace. At the front of the plan is a living room, warmed by a fireplace. Across the central foyer is a cozy study. Two second-floor bedrooms are serviced by two baths. Note the first-floor powder room and storage closet located next to the side entrance. The charm and warmth of this Cape Cod cottage design will be a delight to the family and a practical investment.

Design by
**Home Planners, Inc.**

143

## Design Q3372

First Floor: 1,259 square feet
Second Floor: 942 square feet
Total: 2,201 square feet

● Charm is the key word for this delightful plan's exterior, but don't miss the great floor plan inside. Formal living and dining rooms flank the entry foyer to the front; a family room and breakfast room with beamed ceilings are to the rear. The kitchen and service areas function well together and are near the garage and service entrance for convenience. Upstairs are the sleeping accommodations: two family bedrooms and a master suite of nice proportion.

Design by
Home Planners,
Inc.

**44'-0"**

GARAGE
21⁴ x 21⁴

COVERED
PORCH

FLOWER COURT

SNACK BAR

P'TRY

FAMILY RM.
16⁰x11⁴·BAY

BEDROOM
10⁰ x 11⁶

CL.

KITCHEN
9⁰ x 14⁰

COOK
TOP

BATH

LINEN

OVENS

WOOD
BOX

CL.

DN

LIN.

LIVING RM.
20⁰ x 13⁰

FOYER

UP

CL.

BEDROOM
13⁴x11⁶

CL.

PORCH

**64'-0"**

MASTER
BEDROOM
16⁰x13⁰-18⁴

DESK
BOOKS

PDR.
RM.

BATH

CL.

LIN.

CLIPPED CEILG.

STUDY/
BEDROOM
13⁴x11⁴

WALK-IN
CLOSET

DN

CL.

ROOF

ROOF

ROOF

Design by
Home Planners,
Inc.

## Design Q2145

First Floor: 1,182 square feet
Second Floor: 708 square feet
Total: 1,890 square feet

● Historically referred to as a "half house", this authentic adaptation has its roots in the heritage of New England. With completion of the second floor, the growing family doubles their sleeping capacity. Notice that the overall width of the house is only 44 feet. Take note of the covered porch leading to the garage and the flower court.

## Design Q2146

First Floor: 1,182 square feet
Second Floor: 708 square feet
Total: 1,890 square feet

GARAGE
21⁴ x 21⁴

TERRACE

COVERED PORCH
14⁰ x 12⁰

FLOWER COURT

KITCHEN
9⁰ x 14⁰

FAMILY RM.
16⁰ x 11⁴

BED RM.
10⁰ x 11⁶

BATH

LINEN

LIVING RM.
19⁰ x 13⁰

ENTRY HALL

BED RM.
13⁴ x 11⁶

DESK
BOOKS

PDR. RM.

BATH

CL.

LIN.

CLIPPED CEIL.

MASTER BED RM.
16⁰ x 13⁰

WALK-IN CLOSET

STUDY BED RM.
13⁴ x 11⁴

ROOF

● Historically referred to as a "half house", this authentic adaptation has its roots in the heritage of New England. With completion of the second floor, the growing family doubles its sleeping capacity. Notice that both the family and living rooms have a fireplace. Don't overlook the many built-in units featured throughout the plan.

Design by
Home Planners, Inc.

BED RM.
17⁰ x 10²

MASTER
BED RM.
12²-14⁰ x 17²

ROOF

ROOF

BATH

CL.

HALL

DN.

BED RM.
13⁰ x 11⁶

BATH

DRESSING
RM.

WALK-IN CLOSET

CL.

CL.

ATTIC

ROOF

Design by
Home Planners,
Inc.

74'-0"

TERRACE

FAMILY RM.
29⁴ x 13⁶

EATING

KITCHEN
12⁰ x 15⁶

LAUNDRY
10⁰ x 7⁶

COUNTER

CURB

D.W.

RANGE

REF'S

RAISED HEARTH

32'-0"

DN.

PANTRY

OVEN

SERVICE
ENTRANCE

B.CL.

CL.

PORCH

GARAGE
21⁴ x 23⁴

LIVING RM.
13⁰ x 17⁶

ENTRY

PDR.
RM.

DINING RM.
12⁰ x 15⁶

FENCE

PORCH

# Design Q2596

First Floor: 1,489 square feet
Second Floor: 982 square feet
Total: 2,471 square feet

● A splendid rendition of Cape
Cod styling, this plan is a cozy
space to come home to. An L-
shaped kitchen with island range,
adjacent eating area, and family
room that features a raised-
hearth fireplace and access to a
rear terrace are first-floor highlights. Note, too, the formal dining room, comfy living room,
spacious entry, and sheltered service entrance that leads to an
extra-large laundry room with
additional counter space.
Upstairs are big bedrooms,
including a master suite with a

## Design Q2500

First Floor: 1,851 square feet
Second Floor: 762 square feet
Total: 2,613 square feet

● The large family will enjoy the wonderful living patterns of this charming home. Don't miss the covered rear porch and the many features of the family room. The master suite, conveniently separated from the family bedrooms on the second floor, has its own bath and a huge walk-in closet. Two more giant-sized storage areas—one a linen closet—are found upstairs.

Design by
Home Planners,
Inc.

Design by
Home Planners,
Inc.

## Design Q2563

First Floor: 1,500 square feet
Second Floor: 690 square feet
Total: 2,190 square feet

● This charming Cape Cod will capture your heart with its warm appeal. This home offers you and your family a lot of livability. Upon entering this home, to your left, is a nice-sized living room with fireplace. Adjacent is a dining room. An efficient kitchen and a large, farm kitchen eating area with fireplace will be enjoyed by all. A unique feature on this floor is the master bedroom with a full bath and walk-in closet. Also take notice of the first-floor laundry, the pantry and a study for all of your favorite books. Note the sliding glass doors in the farm kitchen and master bedroom. Upstairs you'll find two bedrooms, one with a walk-in closet. Also here, a sitting room and a full bath are available. Lastly, this design accommodates a three car garage. For information on customizing this design, call 1-800-521-6797, ext. 800.

## Design Q9639
Square Footage: 1,541

● This traditional three-bedroom home projects the appearance of a much larger home. The great room features a cathedral ceiling, fireplace and an arched window above the sliding glass door to the expansive rear deck. The master suite contains a pampering master bath and walk-in closet. Two other bedrooms share a full bath with double bowl vanity.

Design by
Donald A.
Gardner,
Architect, Inc.

**MASTER BED RM.**
11-4 x 14-0

**DECK**
27-6 x 10-0

covered deck

skylights

**GREAT RM.**
15-4 x 18-4

(cathedral ceiling)

fireplace

master bath

walk-in closet

closet

**GARAGE**
21-4 x 20-4

**DINING**
11-4 x 11-0

**BED RM.**
11-4 x 10-0

w d

cl

**FOYER**
6-0 x 6-8

**KITCHEN**
11-4 x 8-4

bath

cl

**BED RM.**
11-4 x 12-9

**PORCH**
18-0 x 5-0

61- 0

51- 5

Design by
Donald A.
Gardner,
Architect, Inc.

## Design Q9620
Square Footage: 1,310

● A multi-paned bay window, dormers, a cupola, a covered porch and a variety of building materials dress up this one-story cottage. The entrance foyer leads to an impressive great room with cathedral ceiling and fireplace. The U-shaped kitchen, adjacent to the dining room, provides an ideal layout for food preparation. An expansive deck offers shelter while admitting cheery sunlight through skylights. A luxurious master bedroom located to the rear of the house takes advantage of the deck area and is assured privacy from two other bedrooms at the front of the house. These family bedrooms share a full bath.

## Design Q2631

First Floor: 1,634 square feet
Second Floor: 1,011 square feet
Total: 2,645 square feet

● Two fireplaces and much more! Notice how all the rooms are accessible from the main hall. That keeps traffic in each room to a minimum, saving you work by preserving your furnishings. There's more. A large family room featuring a beamed ceiling, a fireplace with built-in wood box and double doors onto the terrace. An exceptional U-shaped kitchen is ready to serve you. It has an adjacent breakfast nook. Built-ins, too . . a desk, storage pantry, oven and range. Plus a first floor laundry close at hand.

Design by
Home Planners, Inc.

## Design Q2395

First Floor: 1,481 square feet
Second Floor: 861 square feet
Total: 2,342 square feet

● New England revisited—
the appeal of this type of home
is ageless. As for its livability,
it will serve its occupants
admirably for generations to
come. Besides a giant-sized
formal living room, there is an
equally large family room and
a U-shaped kitchen with
attached eating area. With two
bedrooms downstairs, you
may want to finish off the second floor at a later date.

Design by
Home Planners,
Inc.

## Design Q2699

First Floor: 2,188 square feet
Second Floor: 858 square feet
Total: 3,046 square feet

Design by
Home Planners,
Inc.

## Design Q1718

First Floor: 2,012 square feet
Second Floor: 586 square feet
Total: 2,598 square feet

● This house has everything—an extremely attractive exterior and a fine, working floor plan. Its varying roof lines and arched details at the service entrance and garage doors are fine complements to the shuttered windows and giant chimney stack. The entry leads directly to formal living and dining rooms. The rear of the plan is dominated by casual living in the family room with fireplace and beamed ceiling. The U-shaped kitchen is nearby for convenience. Three bedrooms (or two and a study) are located on this floor and share a full bath. Upstairs is the magnificent master suite. It has its own lounge area, built-in bookcases, walk-in closet and fine bath. Two large storage areas are also found on this floor: one accessed through the master closet and one over the two-car garage.

Design by
Home Planners, Inc.

## Design Q2995

First Floor: 2,465 square feet
Second Floor: 617 square feet
Total: 3,082 square feet

● This New England Colonial delivers beautiful proportions and great livability on 1½ levels. The main area of the house, the first floor, holds a living room, library, family room, dining room and gourmet kitchen. The master bedroom, also on this floor, features a whirlpool tub and sloped ceiling. A long rear terrace stretches the full width of the house. Two bedrooms on the second floor share a full bath; each has a built-in desk.

Design by
Home Planners,
Inc.

Design by
**Home Planners,
Inc.**

BEDROOM
11⁶ x 13⁰

BEDROOM
11⁶ x 15⁶

SKY LIGHT

UPPER SOLARIUM

ATTIC

ATTIC

BATH

ROOF

ROOF

OPEN  LINEN  DESK / VANITY  LINEN

● The exterior detailing of this design recalls 18th-Century New England architecture. Enter by way of the centered front door and you are greeted into the foyer. Directly to the right is the study or optional bedroom or to the left is the living room. This large formal room features sliding glass doors to the sun-drenched solarium. The beauty of the solarium will be appreciated from the master bedroom and the dining room along with the living room.

87'-8"

TERRACE

TERRACE

MASTER BEDROOM
13⁰ x 19⁰

SOLARIUM
14⁰ x 11⁸

DINING RM
12⁰ x 11⁸

KITCHEN
12⁸ x 13⁶

FAMILY RM.
23⁸ x 18⁰

68'-8"

BATH

WALK-IN CLOSET

WALK-IN CLOSET

COVERED PORCH

FLOWER COURT

LIVING RM.
14⁰ x 21⁰

FOYER

PDR RM

PANTRY

STUDY/ BEDROOM
14⁰ x 12⁰

SERVICE HALL

W.R.

BAR

SEAT

LAUNDRY

COVERED PORCH

PORCH

CURB

**Design Q2615**
First Floor: 2,563 square feet
Second Floor: 552 square feet
Total: 3,115 square feet

GARAGE
23⁸ x 24⁰

157

## Design Q9307

Square Footage: 1,948

● Wood and brick details along with an elegant porch highlight the elevation of this special design. A 10-foot-high entry views the open dining room with tapered columns. Gourmet cooks will delight in the island kitchen with pantry and wrapping wet bar/servery. Outdoor access is available from the sunny bayed dinette. In the great room, a cozy fireplace is flanked by large windows with arched transoms above. Two secondary bedrooms share a Hollywood bath with a linen cabinet. At night, the lucky homeowners can retreat to the elegant master suite complete with vaulted ceilings and a pampering master bath. Special amenities include His and Hers vanities, linen closet, corner whirlpool, special shower and roomy walk-in closet. Truly, this home is delightful inside and out.

Design by
**Design
Basics,
Inc.**

# Design Q9308

First Floor: 1,309 square feet
Second Floor: 1,157 square feet
Total: 2,466 square feet

● Sleek lines, Palladian windows and brick and wood detailing create tremendous curb appeal for this four-bedroom, two-story home. Bright windows throughout provide natural warmth and light. A volume entry views three rooms and a dramatic curved stairway. French doors access the family room from the living room with its bright wall of windows and cozy fireplace. The gourmet island kitchen has a pantry, ample counter space and sunny dinette with planning desk in the comfortable breakfast area. Three secondary bedrooms upstairs were designed for family livability. Each has easy access to a roomy bath with dual lavs and a large hall linen closet. A pampering master bedroom includes a cathedral ceiling and breathtaking arched window. In the master bath, who could overlook the walk-in closet, iron-a-way, His and Hers vanities and whirlpool, plus, exquisite window treatments?

Design by
Design
Basics,
Inc.

© design basics inc. 1991

# Design Q9035

Square Footage: 1,341

● Great for narrow lots, this home delivers amazing livability within modest square footage. Notice the efficient U-shaped kitchen with attached dining room. Counter space is abundant for serving and eating. The large family room with fireplace and gambrel ceiling offers an open area that easily accommodates family gatherings and formal entertaining. The three-bedroom sleeping area includes a master suite with full bath and walk-in closet. Bedroom number 3 overlooks the welcoming covered front porch.

Design by
Larry W.
Garnett &
Associates, Inc.

Width 36'–10"
Depth 57'–6"

Bath

Master Bedroom
13'-8" x 11'-8"

Bedroom 2
10' x 11'-4"

Bath 2

Util.

Family Room
16' x 17'
9' Gambrel Clg.

Bedroom 3
13' x 10'

Foyer

Kitchen
16' x 9'

Porch

Dining
11' x 10'

Design by
Larry W.
Garnett &
Associates, Inc.

**Bedroom 3**
13'-8" x 10'

**Bedroom 2**
10' x 11'

**Bath**
2

**Util.**

**Bath**

**Master Bedroom**
11'-8" x 20'
10' Clg.

**Linen**

**French Door**

**Kitchen**
11' x 11'

**Dining**
11' x 11'
Vaulted Clg.

**Hutch**

**Living Room**
17' x 20'
10' Clg.

**Books**

**Porch**

WIDTH 48'-10"
DEPTH 46'-10"

## Design Q9007
Square Footage: 1,669

● With an efficient floor plan and plenty of closet space, this farmhouse is rather economical to build. The simple roof design and well-proportioned bay window and front porch, which are far less costly than many farmhouse designs, allow extras: ten-foot ceilings in the master bedroom and the living room and a unique "gazebo" vaulted ceiling in the dining area. Optional bookcases are located on each side of the fireplace. The laundry room is conveniently located near the bedrooms. The sides and part of the rear of the home are brick veneer, providing for much less maintenance and painting. Plans for a two-car detached garage are included with this design.

Bath

Linen

Bedroom 3
10'-4" x 10'

Kitchen
15' x 10'

Dining
15' x 10'

Bath 2

Master Bedroom
15'-4" x 13'
Cathedral Clg.

Util.

Books

Living Room
20' x 15'-4"
10' Clg.

Books

Books

Design by
Larry W.
Garnett &
Associates, Inc.

Bedroom 2
11'-4" x 13'-8"

Porch

Width 63'-4"
Depth 37'-10"

## Design Q9038
Square Footage: 1,659

● Here's a three-bedroom home with style and comfort that meets family living requirements with less than 2,000 square feet! Gathering areas are accommodated in the living room with built-in bookshelves and fireplace, and the well-planned kitchen/dining area combination. Besides two family bedrooms, there is a lovely master with cathedral ceiling and bath with double vanity. The bay windows, covered front porch and other special design details make this a house to remember.

## Design Q9039
Square Footage: 1,978

● In addition to the wrapping covered front porch of this farmhouse design, there is a second porch to the rear with French-door access to the eating area. Between the two, lies a great floor plan with features often found only in much larger homes: a ten-foot gambrel ceiling in the family room, a large dining room connecting directly to an efficiently planned kitchen, an octagonal breakfast room, and three bedrooms with walk-in closets. Little extras like the bay window in the master bedroom and the double vanity in the master bath make this home a true stand-out.

Design by
Larry W.
Garnett &
Associates, Inc.

Bedroom 3
15'-4" x 11'-8"

Width 54'-2"
Depth 59'-6"

Bedroom 2
10'-8" x 11'-8"

Util.

Porch

Family Room
17'-4" x 20'
10' Gambrel Clg.

French Door

Bath
2

Bath

Breakfast
14' x 10'

Kitchen
13' x 12'

Dining
11'-8" x 12'

Foyer

Master Bedroom
16' x 15'
9' Clg.

Porch

## Design Q9430

First Floor: 1,150 square feet
Second Floor: 543 square feet
Total: 1,693 square feet

● While fitting on some of the smallest lots imaginable, this great 1½-story still encompasses some dynamic features. Check out the dramatic, two-story hearth room that serves as the main living area in the home. Tall windows flank the fireplace and a glass door leads to the outdoor living area. A section of the upper hallway overlooks the hearth room integrating the upper floor with the lower floor. The master bedroom is conveniently located on the main floor overlooking the back yard, with direct access to the full bath serving the lower floor. Two large bedrooms and a bath round out the upper floor.

Design by
**Alan Mascord
Design Associates, Inc.**

## Design Q9476

First Floor: 1,409 square feet
Second Floor: 1,034 square feet
Total: 2,443 square feet

◄ 53' ►

Design by
**Alan Mascord
Design Associates, Inc.**

▲
55'
▼

● A pleasant mix of materials and a columned front porch add visual appeal to a livable floor plan in this exciting two-story design. Living and dining areas on the first floor include a family room with fireplace, living room with bay window, formal dining room and cozy breakfast nook. The den is located just off the entry foyer, away from living areas and noise. Upstairs are three bedrooms including a master suite with full bath. Attic storage over the garage is reached through the second bathroom.

Design by
Larry W.
Garnett &
Associates, Inc.

## Design Q9006

Square Footage: 1,772

● Designed for casual living inside and out, this one-story farmhouse is an ideal family home. The family room features a ten-foot ceiling and a corner fireplace. An enormous dining area can handle even the largest family dinners. The large rear porch is perfect for outdoor entertaining. The laundry room is conveniently located near the three bedrooms. His and Hers walk-in closets and twin lavatories are part of the luxurious master bath. Plans for a 24' x 24' detached garage are included with this design.

Porch
25'-4" x 8'

Master Bedroom
14'-4" x 15'-4"

Bath

Linen

Util.

Bedroom 3
11'-4" x 13'-8"

Dining
17' x 11'-4"

Family Room
17' x 21'-8"
10' Clg.

Bath 2

Kitchen
11' x 13'

Foyer

Bedroom 2
12'-4" x 10'-8"
10' Clg.

Porch

WIDTH 51'-2"
DEPTH 52'-10"

Width 43'-4"
Depth 40'-2"

## Design Q9032
Square Footage: 1,358

● This cozy little farmhouse presents all those special traits that makes it the perfect place to call home. From the covered front porch to the efficient floor plan, this is one that is sure to catch your eye. Living areas to the right of the front entry include a large family room with fireplace, octagonal dining area and U-shaped kitchen with rear yard access. The master bedroom is cleverly separated from two family bedrooms and has its own full bath and a walk-in closet. Note the location of the laundry room—near the bedrooms, the source of dirty clothes.

Design by
Larry W.
Garnett &
Associates, Inc.

# Design Q9608

First Floor: 1,228 square feet
Second Floor: 492 square feet
Total: 1,720 square feet

● An open and spacious interior with the best in up-to-date floor planning offers new excitement in this delightful compact country-style home. Besides the oversized great room with fireplace, there is a wonderful country kitchen incorporating dining space and having access to the sun room for alternate dining and entertaining. The generous master bedroom has its own fireplace and also access to the sun room. A walk-in closet assures plenty of storage space. Upstairs, in addition to two bedrooms sharing a full bath, there is a charming balcony and ample attic storage. A covered porch and a deck — front and rear — add to outdoor lifestyles.

Design by
Donald A.
Gardner,
Architect, Inc.

FRONT

REAR

168

# Design Q9666

First Floor: 1,027 square feet
Second Floor: 580 square feet
Total: 1,607 square feet

● This economical, rustic three-bedroom plan sports a relaxing country image with both front and back covered porches. The openness of the expansive great room to kitchen/dining areas and loft/study areas is reinforced with a shared cathedral ceiling for impressive space. The first level allows for two bedrooms, a full bath and a utility area. The master suite on the second level has a walk-in closet and a master bath with whirlpool tub, shower and double-bowl vanity. The plan is available with a crawl-space foundation.

PORCH
34-4 × 8-0

KIT./DINING
18-0 × 11-8

bath

BED RM.
12-0 × 10-0

w
d

cl

cl

loft above

cl

GREAT RM.
17-4 × 16-4

fireplace

up

BED RM.
12-0 × 12-4

PORCH
34-4 × 8-0

44-8

37-4

LOFT/
STUDY
11-4 × 13-8

STO.
3-4 ×
6-4

master
bath

walk-in
closet

railing

down

great room below

MASTER
BED RM.
12-0 × 14-0

Design by
Donald A.
Gardner,
Architect, Inc.

B-NATHAN.

169

## Design Q2661

First Floor: 1,020 square feet
Second Floor: 777 square feet
Total: 1,797 square feet

● Any other starter house or retirement home couldn't have more charm than this design. Its compact frame houses a very livable plan. An outstanding feature of the first floor is the large country kitchen. Its fine attractions include a beamed ceiling, raised-hearth fireplace, built-in window seat and a door leading to the outdoors. A living room is in the front of the plan and has another fireplace which shares the single chimney. The rear dormered second floor houses the sleeping and bath facilities. For information on customizing this design, call 1-800-521-6797, ext. 800.

Design by
Home Planners,
Inc.

# BRICK OR STONE FARMHOUSES

Though not formally a *style* of Farmhouse, the brick or stone exterior is a popular choice for just about any variation. Because of their solid-looking appearance, brick and stone are used as a statement of permanence, antiquity and heritage. Either may be found as an exterior ingredient; one or both may serve as an accent or embellishment to other exterior sidings. These materials are easy to care for and retain their good looks and durability for many years.

Effective use of brick is accomplished in the Prairie Farmhouse, Design Q9074, where it is used as the primary exterior material. It is complemented by wood railings and wooden shutters at each of the first-floor windows. Also employing brick almost completely throughout the exterior is Design Q9247, a Traditional Farmhouse, borrowing design elements from winged Colonials and Center-Hall designs. Design Q9206, a Modern French-Style Brick, uses brick extensively but heightens the appeal with horizontal wood trim, wooden window trim and wooden trim at the pediment over the garage.

Stone takes on rustically defined proportions in Design Q2527, a Simple Ranch House, and Design Q3351, a Cape Cod Farmhouse, where it is employed in combination with wood siding and other wood design details. A Classic Pennsylvania Stone Farmhouse, Design Q2542, uses stone almost to the exclusion of any other material. Even the chimney stacks are constructed in stone. A French Country House, Design Q9862, presents a unique stone facade with horizontal wood accent at the wing extension. This home is further enhanced by stone chimney stacks and metal-clad roofs over the box window and dining porch.

All of the Farmhouse versions presented, from the basic one-story version to the elaborate two-story country estate, are representative of the sturdiness and long-lasting appeal of brick and stone.

## Design Q9033

Square Footage: 1,528

● Fine farmhouse living takes to one story. In this quaint design, the front porch introduces a fine floor plan. The family room is large and open and acts as a hub for the rest of the home. Nearby is the galley kitchen and a dining area with rear porch access. A fireplace keeps it cozy. Three bedrooms all feature walk-in closets. The master has double sinks in its private bath. Note the utility room with laundry space.

WIDTH 44'-8"
DEPTH 54'-2"

Design by
Larry W.
Garnett &
Associates, Inc.

## Design Q9074 First Floor: 1,288 square feet
Second Floor: 495 square feet; Total: 1,783 square feet

● With its brick-veneer exterior, dormer windows and wraparound porch, this home is a blend of the early 1900s farmhouse and the prairie style. Corner box windows provide a cozy sitting area next to the fireplace in the family room. The efficient kitchen overlooks the breakfast area with its full-length windows. A French door opens to a large covered porch. Double doors open to the master bedroom with a ten-foot gambrel ceiling. The bath features mirrored closet doors and double lavatories. Upstairs, there are two bedrooms, each with dormer window alcoves and sloping ceilings. Plans for a two-car detached garage are included.

Porch

French Door

Window Seat

Breakfast
9' x 8'

Util.

Bath

Kitchen
10' x 12'

Master Bedroom
12' x 15'
10' Gambrel Clg.

Family Room
16' x 21'

Dining
11' x 13'

Porch

Width 44'

Depth 45'

Bath 2

HVAC

Bedroom 2
10' x 12'

Bedroom 3
10' x 12'

Design by
Larry W.
Garnett &
Associates, Inc.

173

# Design Q2805

Square Footage: 1,547

● Compact but completely livable, this one-story home offers the best in country living. From its delightful stone exterior to rear covered porch the look is definitely distinctive. Inside, there's a large living room/dining room area with fireplace and sloped ceiling. It adjoins a breakfast room and U-shaped kitchen for convenient cooking and serving. The bedrooms a located to the front of the plan and include a master bedroor and two family bedrooms (or make one a study or TV room. The main part of the home connects to the two-car garage w a mud room. A huge storage area is found in the garage.

Design by
Home Planners,
Inc.

Design by
Home Planners,
Inc.

# Design Q2527
Square Footage: 2,392

● Vertical boards and battens, field-stone, bay window, a dovecote, a gas lamp and a recessed front entrance are among the appealing exterior features of this U-shaped design. Through the double front doors, flanked by glass side lites, one enters the spacious foyer. Straight ahead is the cozy sunken gathering room with its sloping, beamed ceiling, raised hearth fireplace and two sets of sliding glass doors to the rear terrace. To the right of the foyer is the sleeping wing with its three bedrooms, study (make it the fourth bedroom if you wish) and two baths. To the left is the strategically located powder room and large kitchen with its delightful nook and bay window.

## Design Q2174

First Floor: 1,506 square feet
Second Floor: 1,156 square feet
Total: 2,662 square feet

● Your building budget could
hardly buy more charm, or
greater livability. The appeal
of the exterior is wrapped up
in a myriad of design features.
They include: the interesting
roof lines; the effective use of
brick and horizontal siding; the
delightful window treatment;
the covered front porch; the
chimney and dove-cote
detailing. The livability of the
interior is represented by a
long list of convenient living
features. There is a formal
area consisting of a living room
with fireplace and dining
room. The family room has a
raised hearth fireplace, wood
box and beamed ceiling. Also
on the first floor is a kitchen,
laundry and bedroom with
adjacent bath. Three bedrooms,
lounge and two baths upstairs
plus plenty of closets and bulk
storage over garage. Don't overlook the sliding glass doors,
the breakfast area and the
basement. An excellent plan.

Design by
**Home Planners,
Inc.**

## Design Q2614

First Floor: 1,701 square feet
Second Floor: 1,340 square feet
Total: 3,041 square feet

● Pleasing appearance, with an excellent floor plan. Notice how all the rooms are accessible from a hall. That's a plus for easy housekeeping. Some other extras: an exceptionally large family room which is more than 20' x 15', a gracious living room, formal dining room adjacent to the kitchen/nook area, four large bedrooms, a secluded guest suite plus a huge storage area.

Note that the large guest suite, featuring a full bath, is only accessible by the back stairs in the family room. You could use it as a spacious library, playroom, or a hobby area. Two fireplaces (one with a built-in wood box), walk-in closets, covered front porch and rear terrace also highlight this home.

Design by
Home Planners,
Inc.

## Design Q9206

First Floor: 1,421 square feet
Second Floor: 578 square feet
Total: 1,999 square feet

● Growing families will love this unique plan which combines all the essentials with an abundance of stylish touches. Start with the living areas — a spacious great room with high ceilings, windows overlooking the back yard, a through-fireplace to the kitchen and access to the rear yard. A dining room with hutch space accommodates formal occasions. The hearth kitchen features a well-planned work area and a bay-windowed breakfast area. The master suite with whirlpool and walk-in closet is found downstairs while three family bedrooms are upstairs.

Design by
Design
Basics,
Inc.

© 1990 design basics inc.

## Design Q9247

First Floor: 1,297 square feet
Second Floor: 558 square feet
Total: 1,855 square feet

● Here's the perfect family plan with loads of livability. Go beyond the front covered porch and you'll find a thoughtful floor plan. A formal dining room with large boxed window is a complement to the great room with handsome fireplace and tall windows. A snack bar, pantry, two lazy Susans and planning desk grace the kitchen/breakfast room area. The master suite is conveniently located on the first floor and features a boxed window and well-appointed bath. Three family bedrooms upstairs share a full bath. Note the volume ceiling above the arched window in bedroom 4.

Design by
Design
Basics,
Inc.

179

# Design Q9309

First Floor: 1,506 square feet
Second Floor: 633 square feet
Total: 2,139 square feet

● Graceful lines and arched windows create a delightful country flair for this 1½-story home. From the volume entry, there's a clear view of the stunning great room enhanced by the handsome fireplace and windows with a view. The adjacent dining room is perfect for entertaining. A dinette, open to the island kitchen, allows sunlight to brighten and warm this family-sized eating area. The covered patio is accessed from the dinette. In the gourmet kitchen, convenience is evident through features such as a snack bar, planning desk and walk-in pantry. The main-floor master suite sports a beautiful arched window, double doors and sloped ceiling. A two-person whirlpool, His and Hers vanities and a decorator plant ledge complement the master dressing area. Three secondary bedrooms upstairs share a hall bath.

Design by
Design
Basics,
Inc.

© 1990 design basics inc.

180

## Design Q9219

First Floor: 1,132 square feet
Second Floor: 1,087 square feet
Total: 2,219 square feet

● The detailed front porch, attractive chimney and overall pleasing exterior make this home a delight in any neighborhood. The interior features a floor plan for active families. The front dining room includes a formal, tiered ceiling and hutch space. The great room with fireplace and ten-foot ceiling provides multi-purpose living space. The ample kitchen includes a breakfast room with bay window. The highlight of the four-bedroom sleeping area is the master suite with elegant vaulted ceiling and skylit bath with whirlpool.

© 1988 design basics inc.

Design by
Design
Basics,
Inc.

## Design Q3356

First Floor: 1,610 square feet
Second Floor: 1,200 square feet
Total: 2,810 square feet

● Traditionally speaking, this home takes blue ribbons. Its family room has a raised-hearth fireplace and there's a covered porch reached through sliding glass doors for informal eating. The living room also has a fireplace and is near the boxed-windowed dining room. A large clutter room off the garage could be turned into a hobby or sewing room. Four bedrooms on the second floor include a master suite with His and Hers walk-in closets and three family bedrooms.

Design by
Home Planners,
Inc.

# Design Q3351

First Floor: 1,794 square feet
Second Floor: 887 square feet
Total: 2,681 square feet

● Home-grown comfort is the key to the appeal of this traditionally styled home. From the kitchen with attached family room to the living room with fireplace and attached formal dining room, this plan has it all. Notice the first-floor master bedroom with whirlpool tub and adjacent study. A nearby powder room turns the study into a convenient guest room. On the second floor are three more bedrooms with ample closet space and a full bath. The two-car garage has a large storage area.

Design by
Home Planners,
Inc.

Design by
Home Planners,
Inc.

## Design Q3502

First Floor: 2,086 square feet
Second Floor: 2,040 square feet
Total: 4,126 square feet

● This lovely stone farmhouse is reminiscent of the solid, comfortable homes once so prevalent on homesteads throughout America. The columned front porch leads to a formal foyer with living room on the left and library on the right. The formal dining room connects directly to the living room and indirectly to the island kitchen through a butler's pantry. The family room and breakfast room have beamed ceilings and are both open to the kitchen. A covered veranda is accessed from the breakfast room and leads to a side yard. On the second floor are three bedrooms and a guest room with private bath. The master bedroom has a fireplace and a fine bath with separate shower and whirlpool tub. Two walk-in closets grace the dressing area. The two secondary bedrooms share a full bath with double vanity.

## Design Q2542 First Floor: 2,025 square feet
## Second Floor: 1,726 square feet; Total: 3,751 square feet

Design by
**Home Planners,
Inc.**

Here is a fieldstone Farmhouse that has its roots in the rolling countryside of Pennsylvania. In addition to its stone exterior, the charm of such a house is characterized by the various appendages. These additions, of course, came into being as the size of the family fortune increased. The living potential offered by this farmhouse adaptation can hardly be topped. Imagine, five fireplaces! Study the outstanding livability offered in this house from the past. Surely its floor plan has been up-dated to serve today's contemporary family.

Copyright 1992 Stephen S. Fuller, Inc.

## Design Q9862

Square Footage: 2,170

● This classic cottage features a stone and wooden exterior with an arch-detailed porch and box bay window. From the foyer, double doors open to the den with built-in bookcases and a fireplace. A full bath is situated next to the den, allowing for an optional guest room. The family room is centrally located, just beyond the foyer. Its hearth is framed by windows overlooking the porch at the rear of the home. The master bedroom opens onto the rear porch. The master bath, with large walk-in closet, double vanities, corner tub and separate shower completes this relaxing retreat. Left of the family room awaits a sun room with access to the covered porch. A breakfast area complements the attractive and efficiently-designed kitchen. A short hallway from the sun room leads to two bedrooms with large closets and shared full bath featuring double vanities.

Design by
**Design Traditions**
Atlanta

BEDROOM NO. 3
11'-6" X 11'-0"

BATH

BEDROOM NO. 2
11'-4" X 11'-0"

SUN ROOM
12'-0" X 13'-8"

PORCH

MASTER BATH

W.I.C.

PORCH

BREAKFAST
10'-0" X 9'-0"

FAMILY ROOM
18'-0" X 14'-0"

MASTER BEDROOM
13'-4" X 15'-6"

LAUNDRY

KITCHEN
12'-0" X 13'-2"

BATH

STORAGE

DN

DINING ROOM
11'-4" X 11'-4"

FOYER
6'-8" X 11'-10"

DEN/GUEST BEDROOM
11'-4" X 14'-0"

TWO CAR GARAGE
20'-4" X 19'-8"

PORCH

Width 62'-4"
Depth 62'-2"

Copyright 1992 Stephen S. Fuller

## Design Q9861

First Floor: 1,960 square feet
Second Floor: 965 square feet
Total: 2,925 square feet

The facade of this charming home is Americana at its best with a rocking-chair porch, bay window and dormers above, finished in stone and wood siding and faithfully detailed. A convenient outdoor entrance to the two-car garage is located to the right of the front porch. The main level features an easy flow, beginning with the dining room to the right of the foyer. A hallway between the foyer and main staircase helps to promote a sense of openness. The great room features a large hearth and French doors to the patio, and leads directly to the breakfast area and kitchen. Storage closets and a counter-top desk area highlight the kitchen which, along with the laundry room, is conveniently located to the rear of the home. Left of the foyer is an attractive study with a large bay window. The master suite, featuring a bay-windowed sitting area, large master bath with double vanities and shower and ample closet space, completes the main level. On the upper level, bedroom two features a full bath and has three dormer windows overlooking the front lawn. The third and fourth bedrooms share another full bath.

Design by
**Design Traditions
Atlanta**

Width: 64'-11"
Depth: 51'-11"

## Design Q2633

First Floor: 1,338 square feet
Second Floor: 1,200 square feet
Third Floor: 506 square feet
Total: 3,044 square feet

● This is certainly a pleasing Georgian. Its facade features a front porch with a roof supported by 12'' diameter wooden columns. The garage wing has a sheltered service entry and brick facing which complements the design. Sliding glass doors link the terrace and family room, providing an indoor/outdoor area for entertaining as pictured in the rear elevation. The floor plan has been designed to serve the family efficiently. The stairway in the foyer leads to four second-floor bedrooms. The third floor is windowed and can be used as a studio and study.

Design by
**Home Planners,**
**Inc.**

This two-story farmhouse brings [to mi]nd the stone houses of Bucks [Coun]ty, Pa. The recessed center [entra]nce opens to the foyer. To the [left i]s the living room with its adja[cent] music alcove. The sunken [study] offers a guest retreat. The effi[cient], U-shaped kitchen functions

with the large breakfast room [and] separate dining room with fire[plac]e. The three bedroom upstairs [featu]res nice sized rooms and a [bath] fireplace. Note the laundry.

### Design Q2976

First Floor: 1,787 square feet
Second Floor: 1,260 square feet
Total: 3,047 square feet

Design by
Home Planners,
Inc.

Design by
Home Planners,
Inc.

## Design Q2223 First Floor: 1,266 square feet
Second Floor: 1,232 square feet; Total: 2,498 square feet

● The appealing double front doors of this home open wide to fine livability for the large, growing family. The spacious entrance hall is flanked by the formal, end living room and the all-purpose, beamed ceiling family room. Both rooms have a commanding fire-place. The U-shaped kitchen overlooks the rear yard and is but a step, or two, from the breakfast nook and the formal dining room. The mud room controls the flows of traffic during the inclement weather. Observe the laundry equipment and the washroom. Five bedrooms, two full baths, and plenty of closets are what make the second floor truly outstanding. There are a number of other convenient living features that make this design distinctive. How many of these can you list?

# CONTEMPORARY FARMHOUSES

Seemingly diverse, the notions of *contemporary* and *farmhouse* blend surprisingly well. In the Contemporary Farmhouse, design takes a classic 1½- or two-story farmhouse structure and modifies it with more rounded, open or vaulted forms.

The style may have begun in the West, particularly California and the Pacific Coast, and spread eastward to the Midwest, South and East—in direct opposition to traditional farmhouse evolution.

Wood, stone and glass are the major components of the style and afford it a contemporary look and ambience. The contemporary use of glass gives the style its characteristic open-air, light-filled properties. The open floor plans that are usually contained in these homes allow for easy traffic patterns and great indoor/outdoor livability.

Many fine examples of this divergent style are presented. Designs Q9260 and Q9235 represent the Modern Midwest Wood style and take their forms and feeling from traditional dwellings popular in the Midwest. Adding a more contemporary feel, however, are the arched details, half-round windows and the clean, simple lines. More reminiscent of the Pacific Northwest are designs such as Q9480 which stands tall and upright and features French-styled rooflines. The arched window in the foyer is repeated in the bonus room over the garage. In the best Southern tradition are two designs, Q9600 and Q9619, which feature contemporary additions such as the skylit sun rooms and the lovely rear decks. Maintaining traditional appeal, however, is the chimney cap on Design Q9619. Designs Q3471 and Q3438 are exquisite echoes of the Tin-Roof or Shed-Roof style but are often referred to as the California Farmhouse or California Contemporary Farmhouse. Each has the bold statement of contemporary design, yet keeps a rustic sense. Both floor plans are open and spacious in the best contemporary style. Blending the best elements of traditional and contemporary details, Design Q2931 can be classified as a Transitional home. Resembling a Cape Cod, with winged extensions and multi-paned windows, it also incorporates large patio areas and vertical wood siding, giving it a contemporary accent.

The Contemporary Farmhouses in this section represent an entirely new and exciting form for the standard country residence. Though perhaps not for the farmhouse purist, these evolved designs provide a wonderful option for those who love the fluidity of contemporary form and the grace of traditional style.

## Design Q3466

quare Footage: 1,800

● Small but inviting, this one-story ranch-style farm-house is the perfect choice for a small family or empty-nesters. It's loaded with amenities even the most particular homeowner can appreciate. For example, the living room and dining room each have plant shelves, sloped ceilings and built-ins to enhance livability. The living room also sports a warming hearth. The master bedroom contains a well-appointed bath with dual vanity and walk-in closet. The additional bedroom has its own bath with linen storage. The kitchen is separated from the breakfast nook by a clever bar area. Access to the two-car garage is through a laundry area with washer/dryer hookup space. For information on customizing this design, call 1-800-521-6797, ext. 800.

Design by
Home Planners,
Inc.

## Design Q3471

First Floor: 3,166 square feet
Second Floor: 950 square feet
Guest Living Area: 680 square feet
Total: 4,796 square feet

Width 154'
Depth 94'-8"

Design by
Home Planners,
Inc.

● Western farmhouse style living is captured in this handsome design. The central entrance leads into a cozy parlor—half walls provide a view of the grand dining room. Entertaining is a cinch with the dining room's built-in china alcove, service counter and fireplace. The country kitchen, with large island cooktop, overlooks the gathering room with its full wall of glass. The master bedroom will satisfy even the most discerning tastes. It boasts a raised hearth, porch access and master bath with walk-in closet, separate vanities and whirlpool. You may want to use one of the additional first-floor bedrooms as a study, the other as a guest room. To round out the first floor, you'll also find a clutter room with pantry, freezer space and access to storage space. Two family bedrooms and attic storage make up the second floor. Note, too, the separate garage and guest house which make this such a winning design.

## Design Q3438

First Floor: 1,489 square feet
Second Floor: 741 square feet
Total: 2,230 square feet

● A unique farmhouse plan which provides a
grand floor plan, this home is comfortable in
country or suburban settings. Formal entertaining areas share first-floor space with family
gathering rooms and work and service areas.
The master suite is also on this floor for convenience and privacy. Upstairs is a guest bedroom, private bath and loft area that makes a
perfect studio. Special features make this a
great place to come home to.

Design by
Home Planners,
Inc.

## Design Q3443

First Floor: 1,211 square feet
Second Floor: 614 square feet
Total: 1,825 square feet

Design by
Home Planners,
Inc.

● What a pampering retreat! The master suite
in this house is on a level all its own. The 21-foot
bedroom includes a sitting area. The master bath
features a walk-in closet, dual vanities, separate tub
and shower and a compartmented toilet. A second
bedroom or optional den, with a full bath nearby,
is located on the first floor. The formal living and
dining room have sloped ceilings separated by a
plant shelf and bay windows. The family room
features a snack bar to the kitchen and patio access.
Tiled floors throughout add a special touch. Note the
hobby shop in the garage. For information on customizing this design, call 1-800-521-6797, ext. 800.

## Design Q3469

First Floor: 1,066 square feet
Second Floor: 1,006 square feet
Total: 2,072 square feet

● Our neo-classic farmhouse offers plenty of room for delightful diversions; a sheet-metal roof adds old-fashioned flair; front and rear porches accommodate out-of-doors lounging. Inside, a large living area with fireplace affords grand lounging; a dining room, cozy interludes. A fully functional kitchen, powder room and utility room round out the first floor. The second floor provides well-arranged sleeping quarters—with large master bedroom— and two full baths. Don't forget the interesting mud yard separating the garage from the house.

WIDTH 70'-4"
DEPTH 50'-4"

Design by
Home Planners, Inc.

WIDTH 85'-2"
DEPTH 49'-2"

Design by
Home Planners,
Inc.

## Design Q3468

First Floor: 1,618 square feet
Second Floor: 510 square feet
Total: 2,128 square feet

● There's nothing lacking in this contemporary farmhouse. A wraparound porch ensures a favorite spot for enjoying good weather. A large great room sports a fireplace and lots of natural light. Grab a snack at the kitchen island/snack bar or in the bright breakfast room. The vaulted foyer grandly introduces the dining room and sitting parlor—the master bedroom is just off this room. Inside it: tray ceiling, fireplace, luxury bath and walk-in closet. Stairs lead up to a quaint loft/bedroom—perfect for study or snoozing—a full bath and an additional bedroom. Designated storage space also makes this one a winner.

## Design Q9312

First Floor: 1,150 square feet
Second Floor: 1,120 square feet
Total: 2,270 square feet

● Lap siding, special windows and a covered porch enhance the elevation of this popular style. The spacious two-story entry surveys the formal dining room with hutch space. An entertainment center, through-fireplace and bayed windows add appeal to the great room. Families will love the spacious kitchen, breakfast and hearth room. Enhancements to this casual living area include a through-fireplace, gazebo dinette, wrapping counters, an island kitchen and planning desk. An efficient U-shaped staircase routes traffic throughout. Comfortable secondary bedrooms and a sumptuous master suite feature privacy by design. Bedroom 3 is highlighted by a half round window, volume ceiling and double closets while Bedroom 4 features a built-in desk. The master suite has a vaulted ceiling, large walk-in closet, His and Hers vanities, compartmented stool/shower area and an oval whirlpool tub.

© design basics inc. 1991

Design by
Design
Basics,
Inc.

## Design Q9480

First Floor: 1,921 square feet
Second Floor: 1,417 square feet
Total: 3,338 square feet
Bonus Room: 608 square feet

● Here's a farmhouse for a large family. The covered porch at the entry wraps all the way around to the side for great outdoor living. Inside you'll find a formal parlor with bay window, dining room with box window, den with built-in shelves and a family room with fireplace and wet bar. The nook is octagonal and allows casual meals from the L-shaped island kitchen. The three-car garage is reached through the laundry area. There is also a rear staircase here to the second floor. Four bedrooms reside on the upper level. Included are a luxurious master suite with huge walk-in closet and three family bedrooms sharing a full bath. Additional storage space or room for future development sits over the garage.

Design by
**Alan Mascord
Design Associates, Inc.**

◄ 91' ►

Grt. rm.
18¹ x 14⁰

Bfst.
10⁰ x 12⁵

Kit.
8¹⁰ x 11³

DESK

Din.
10⁰ x 12⁴

Gar.
21³ x 21⁸

COVERED PORCH

40'-0"

44'-0"

© 1990 design basics inc.

## Design Q9260

First Floor: 891 square feet
Second Floor: 759 square feet
Total: 1,650 square feet

● A quaint covered porch leads to a volume entry with decorator plant ledge above the closet in this home. The formal dining room has a boxed window that can be seen from the entry. A fireplace in the large great room adds warmth and coziness to the attached breakfast room and well-planned kitchen. Notice the nearby powder room for guests. Upstairs are three bedrooms. Bedroom 3 has a beautiful arched window under a volume ceiling. The master bedroom has a walk-in closet and pampering dressing area with double vanity and a whirlpool under a window. The upstairs landing overlooks the entry below.

Design by
Design
Basics,
Inc.

Br. 2
10⁰ x 11⁶

W/P

Mbr.
12⁰ x 16⁰

LIN.

9'-0" CLG.

DN

10'-0" CLG.

OPEN TO BELOW

Br. 3
10⁰ x 11⁰

PLANTS

## Design Q9235

First Floor: 919 square feet
Second Floor: 927 square feet
Total: 1,846 square feet

● Wonderful country design begins with the wraparound porch of this plan. Explore further and find a two-story entry with a coat closet and plant shelf above and a strategically placed staircase alongside. The island kitchen with a boxed window over the sink is adjacent to a large bay-windowed dinette. The great room includes many windows and a fireplace. A powder bath and laundry room are both conveniently placed on the first floor. Upstairs, the large master suite contains His and Hers walk-in closets, corner windows and a bath area featuring a double vanity and whirlpool tub. Two pleasant secondary bedrooms have interesting angles and a third bedroom in the front features a volume ceiling and arched window.

Design by
Design
Basics,
Inc.

© 1989 design basics inc.

BEDROOM
10⁴ x 14⁰
+ DORMER

DESK  BOOK'S  DESK

HALL

BEDROOM
11⁸ x 14⁰
+ DORMER

LINEN

DN

BATH

RAILING

OPEN TO
FOYER BELOW

LEDGE  LEDGE

65'-0"

47'-0"

RAILING

WOOD DECK

DN

FAMILY
KITCHEN
12² x 21⁴

MASTER
SUITE
16⁴ x 11⁴

BATH

RAILING

WOOD DECK

DN

SINK

DW

W.I.C.

STORAGE

D W LT BC
LAUNDRY

RANGE

REFG

DN

PDR

LINEN

DN

RAILING

UP

DINING
12² x 10⁴

FOYER
HIGH
CEILING

LIVING
11⁸ x 14⁰

CURB

GARAGE
20⁰ x 22⁰

COVERED PORCH

RAILING

RAILING

UP

## Design Q3467

First Floor: 1,276 square feet
Second Floor: 658 square feet
Total: 1,934 square feet

● Bold and beautiful, this
Neo-classic farmhouse will
delight family and friends alike.
Lap wood siding combined
with a standing seam metal
roof provides a wealth of visual
appeal. Inside, living takes off
with a great kitchen and family
room combination. Or take
in brunch on the wood deck
located just off this area. For
more formal occasions, a split
dining room and living room—
with a fireplace—will serve
well. A covered wraparound
porch is accessible from both
rooms and makes outdoor
living a pleasure. Located at the
rear of the first floor, the master
bedroom extends the finest
accommodations including a
private bath and a walk-in closet. Upstairs, two bedrooms with
dormers will comfortably lodge
family and guests. For information on customizing this design
call 1-800-521-6797, ext. 800.

Design by
Home Planners,
Inc.

## Design Q9458

First Floor: 1,730 square feet
Second Floor: 1,215 square feet
Total: 2,945 square feet
Bonus Room: 462 square feet

● Though its facade says country casual, this home has a floor plan that is as elegant and modern as any. The front porch wraps around a formal farmhouse parlor with bay window. This room is almost completely open to the foyer and sits right next to the more private den. The large family room features a vaulted ceiling and fireplace. It blends into the bay-windowed nook adjacent to the L-shaped island kitchen. A powder room separates the space between the kitchen and formal dining room with boxed window. Up an open staircase is the four-bedroom second floor. Three family bedrooms share a full bath. The master suite has a vaulted ceiling, large walk-in closet and bath with spa.

Design by
**Alan Mascord
Design Associates, Inc.**

## Design Q9600

Square Footage: 2,053

● This three-bedroom country cottage with sun room at the front takes advantage of south-facing lots. The generous entry foyer allows direct access to the great room, dining room and sun room. A country kitchen with breakfast bar and cooking island provides an abundance of cabinet space. Split away from two family bedrooms is a private master suite with walk-in closets and master bath with whirlpool tub, shower and double-bowl vanity. The great room has direct access to a deck and the sun room. Both the great room and sun room have cathedral ceilings (note skylights in the sun room). A covered breezeway connects the house to the garage. The house is built on a crawlspace foundation.

REAR

Design by
**Donald A. Gardner, Architect, Inc.**

FRONT

REAR

# Design Q9619

Square Footage: 2,021

● Multi-paned windows, shutters, dormers, bay windows and a delightful covered porch grace the facade of this country cottage. Inside, the floor plan is no less appealing. Note that the great room has a fireplace, cathedral ceiling and sliding glass doors with an arched window above to allow for natural illumination of the room. A sun room with hot tub leads to an adjacent deck. This space can also be reached from the master bath. The generous master bedroom has a walk-in closet and spacious bath with double bowl vanity, shower and garden tub. Two additional bedrooms are located at the other end of the house for privacy. The garage is connected to the house by a breezeway.

Design by
Donald A. Gardner, Architect, Inc.

GARAGE
20-4 x 20-4

DECK
36-8 x 10-0

covered breezeway

SUN RM.
15-8 x 7-10

hot tub

GREAT RM.
20-0 x 15-6
(cathedral ceiling)

fireplace

UTILITY
9-0 x 5-4

wash
dry

bath

powder rm.

lin.

cl

BED RM.
11-4 x 13-8

walk-in closet

master bath

rail

FOYER
4-6 x 12-4

DINING
12-0 x 12-0

KITCHEN
14-4 x 12-0

cl

cl

BED RM.
14-8 x 11-0

MASTER
BED RM.
13-4 x 16-8

cl

PORCH
19-2 x 5-0

BRKFST.
13-4 x 7-8

67-4

67-6

FRONT

## Design Q9647
Square Footage: 2,413

● Multi-paned windows, dormers, a covered porch and two projected windows with shed roofs offer a welcoming front exterior to this wonderful one-story home. The great room with cathedral ceiling, paddle fan, built-in cabinets and bookshelves has direct access to the sun room through two sliding glass doors. Columns between the foyer and great room create a dramatic entrance to the great room. The kitchen and cooking island serve both the dining room and breakfast area as well as the great room via a pass-through. The master suite has a double-door entrance and cathedral ceiling and overlooks the rear deck through a sliding glass door. Three family bedrooms and two baths are found at the other end of the house for privacy. The front bedroom could double as a study. The two-car garage contains ample storage space.

Design by
Donald A.
Gardner,
Architect, Inc.

DECK
28-6 × 10-0

seat

SUN RM.
16-0 × 8-0

DINING
11-4 × 11-10

wash dry

storage

BED RM.
11-4 × 10-0

fireplace

GREAT RM.
18-0 × 14-0
(cathedral ceiling)

KIT.
11-4 × 8-0

GARAGE
21-0 × 21-0

cl

cl

cl

bath

bath

FOYER
7-4 × 5-8

MASTER
BED RM.
11-4 × 14-0

cl

cl

cl

lin

cl

PORCH
16-0 × 5-4

BED RM.
11-4 × 11-0

42-4

71-0

Design by
Donald A.
Gardner,
Architect, Inc.

## Design Q9604

Square Footage: 1,506

● This unusual compact house maximizes its use of living areas and offers features found mostly only in larger house plans. A lovely facade, adorned with multi-paned windows, shutters, dormers, bay windows and a covered porch, gives way to a truly livable floor plan. The great room with cathedral ceiling, fireplace, paddle fan, built-in cabinets and bookshelves has direct access to the sun room through two sliding glass doors. Decorative columns between the foyer and great room create a dramatic entrance. Sleeping accommodations include a master with ample closet space and two family bedrooms. Note the split-bedroom plan configuration —providing utmost privacy.

Floor plan labels:

65 – 2

74 – 8

DECK

cabinets
fireplace

skylights

tub

cl

GREAT RM.
15-4 × 19-6
(cathedral ceiling)

master
bath

lin.

MASTER
BED RM.
16-0 × 13-4

SUN RM.
12-6 × 9-0

cl    cl

BRKFST.
9-4 × 9-6

KIT.
12-6 ×13-0

DINING
12-0 ×12-8

FOYER
5-0 ×13-0

cl

lin.

optional opening

BED RM./
STUDY
11-4 × 10-4

bath

cl

UTILITY

wash dry

PORCH

BED RM.
13-0 × 12-0

GARAGE
21-10 × 23-0

Design by
Donald A.
Gardner,
Architect, Inc.

## Design Q9670
Square Footage: 2,046

● This three-bedroom country cottage projects an intriguing appearance with its bay windows, dormers and L-shaped layout. The great room has a cathedral ceiling along with an arched window above the exterior door leading to the deck. The sun room with operable skylights is accessible from the great room, kitchen and deck for maximum exposure. The centrally located kitchen allows direct access to eating and living areas. Three bedrooms include a master suite and a bedroom that might also be useful as a study.

## Design Q9601

Square Footage: 1,988

● This country-style ranch is the essence of excitement with its combination of exterior building materials and interesting shapes. Because it is angled, it allows for flexibility in design—the great room and/or the family room can be lengthened to meet family space requirements. The master bedroom has a cathedral ceiling, a walk-in closet, private deck and a spacious master bath with whirlpool tub. There are three family bedrooms, two of which share a full bath and one having a private bath. Expansive deck area with space for a hot tub wraps around interior family gathering areas. Both family room and great room have cathedral ceilings; the great room has a fireplace. For crawl-space foundation, order Design Q9601; for partial basement foundation, order Design Q9601-A.

Design by
Donald A.
Gardner,
Architect, Inc.

wood lattice above

seat

**DECK**
28-8 x 16-4

down

hot tub

down

**MASTER BED RM.**
13-4 x 16-0
fireplace

skylights

**KIT.**
8-8 x
11-10

ref.

**BED RM.**
12-0 x 16-0
fireplace

44-0

tub

master bath

clerestory above

fireplace

walk-in closet

**GREAT RM.**
20-0 x 21-0
exposed wood beams

cl

bath

walk-in closet

**FOYER**

lin

wash dry

down

**PORCH**
27-8 x 6-0

down

65-4

# Design Q9607
Square Footage: 1,299

● Though rustic in appearance, this two-bedroom plan provides all the features sought after in today's well-planned home. A large central area includes a great room, entrance foyer and kitchen with serving and eating counter. Note the use of cathedral ceilings with exposed wood beams, skylights, clerestory windows and fireplace in this area. The master suite has an optional fireplace, walk-in closet, and whirlpool tub. The second bedroom also has an optional fireplace and a full bath. All rooms open to the rear deck, which supplies space for a hot tub.

Design by
Donald A.
Gardner,
Architect, Inc.

REAR

FRONT

## Design Q9609
Square Footage: 1,426

● Rustic charm abounds in this amenity-filled three-bedroom plan. From the central living area with cathedral ceiling and fireplace to the sumptuous master suite, there are few features omitted. Be sure to notice the large walk-in closet in the master bedroom, the pampering whirlpool tub, and separate water-closet compartment. Two other bedrooms have a connecting bath with single-bowl vanity for each. The house wraps around a screened porch with skylights — a grand place for eating and entertaining. The spacious rear deck has plenty of room for a hot tub.

Design by
Donald A.
Gardner,
Architect, Inc.

REAR

FRONT

TERRACE

STUDY
12⁶ x 16⁰

GATHERING RM.
16⁶ x 16⁶

MASTER
BEDROOM
14⁰ x 16⁰

DINING RM.
11⁸ x 10⁸

SLOPED CEILING

SLOPED CEILING

CL.

LINEN

BAR  S.

TERRACE

SLOPED

BRKFST. RM.
11⁸ x 10⁸

DRESSING RM.

WALK-IN
CLOSET

BATH

SLOPED CEILING

CL.

DN.

DESK

PASS THRU

CL.

VANITY

BATH

CL.

FOYER

CIR. CLOS.

RAILING

LAV'TRY

KITCHEN
11⁸ x 10⁰

OVENS

SEAT

WHIRLPOOL

S.

BEDROOM
12⁴ x 12⁶

COVERED
PORCH

LAUND

CL.

REF'G

COOK
TOP

DW

COURTYARD

CURB

GARAGE
21⁴ x 21⁴

STORAGE

63'-0

64'-4"

Design by
**Home Planners,
Inc.**

# Design Q2931
Square Footage: 2,032

● Little details make the difference in this charming showplace: picket-fenced courtyard, carriage lamp, window boxes, shutters, muntined windows, multi-gabled roof, cornice returns, vertical and horizontal siding with corner board, front door with glass side lites, etc. Inside this appealing exterior there is a truly outstanding floor plan for the small family or empty-nesters. The master bedroom suite is long on luxury with a separate dressing room, private vanities, and whirlpool bath. An adjacent study, with warming fireplace, is just the right retreat. Other attractions: roomy kitchen and breakfast area, spacious gathering room, rear and side terraces, and an attached two-car garage with storage. For information on customizing this design, call 1-800-521-6797, ext. 800.

## Design Q2947
Square Footage: 1,830

**Design by**
**Home Planners, Inc.**

● This charming one-story traditional home greets visitors with a covered porch. A uniquely shaped galley-style kitchen shares a snack bar with the spacious gathering room where a fireplace is the focal point. The dining room has sliding glass doors to the rear terrace as does the master suite. This bedroom area also includes a luxury bath with whirlpool tub and separate dressing room. Two additional bedrooms, one that could double as a study, are located at the front of the home. The two-car garage features a large storage area and can be reached through the service entrance to the home or from the rear terrace. For information on customizing this design, call 1-800-521-6797, ext. 800. California Engineered Plans and California Stock Plans are available for this home. Call 1-800-521-6797 for more information.

# When You're Ready To Order . . .

## Let Us Show You Our Home Blueprint Package.

Building a home? Planning a home? Our Blueprint Package contains nearly everything you need to get the job done right, whether you're working on your own or with help from an architect, designer, builder or subcontractors. Each Blueprint Package is the result of many hours of work by licensed architects or professional designers.

## QUALITY

Hundreds of hours of painstaking effort have gone into the development of your blueprint set. Each home has been quality-checked by professionals to insure accuracy and buildability.

## VALUE

Because we sell in volume, you can buy professional-quality blueprints at a fraction of their development cost. With our plans, your dream home design costs only a few hundred dollars, not the thousands of dollars that custom architects charge.

## SERVICE

Once you've chosen your favorite home plan, you'll receive fast efficient service whether you choose to mail your order to us or call us toll free at 1-800-521-6797.

## SATISFACTION

Our years of service to satisfied home plan buyers provide us the experience and knowledge that guarantee your satisfaction with our product and performance.

## ORDER TOLL FREE 1-800-521-6797

After you've studied our Blueprint Package and Important Extras on the following pages, simply mail the accompanying order form on page 221 or call toll free on our Blueprint Hotline: 1-800-521-6797. We're ready and eager to serve you.

Each set of blueprints is an interrelated collection of floor plans, interior and exterior elevations, dimensions, cross-sections, diagrams and notations showing precisely how your house is to be constructed.

## *Here's what you get:*

### Frontal Sheet
This artist's sketch of the exterior of the house, done in realistic perspective, gives you an idea of how the house will look when built and landscaped. Large ink-line floor plans show all levels of the house and provide a quick overview of your new home's livability, as well as a handy reference for studying furniture placement.

### Foundation Plan
Drawn to 1/4-inch scale, this sheet shows the complete foundation layout including support

walls, excavated and unexcavated areas, if any, and foundation notes. If slab construction rather than basement, the plan shows footings and details for a monolithic slab. This page, or another in the set, also includes a sample plot plan for locating your house on a building site.

### Detailed Floor Plans
Complete in 1/4-inch scale, these plans show the layout of each floor of the house. All rooms and interior spaces are carefully dimensioned and keys are provided for cross-section details given later in the plans. The positions of all electrical outlets and switches are clearly shown.

### House Cross-Sections
Large-scale views, normally drawn at 3/8-inch equals 1 foot, show sections or cut-aways of the foundation, interior walls, exterior walls,

floors, stairways and roof details. Additional cross-sections are given to show important changes in floor, ceiling or roof heights or the relationship of one level to another. Extremely valuable for construction, these sections show exactly how the various parts of the house fit together.

### Interior Elevations
These large-scale drawings show the design and placement of kitchen and bathroom cabinets, laundry areas, fireplaces, bookcases and other built-ins. Little "extras," such as mantelpiece and wainscoting drawings, plus moulding sections, provide details that give your home that custom touch.

### Exterior Elevations
Drawings in 1/4-inch scale show the front, rear and sides of your house and give necessary notes on exterior materials and finishes. Particular attention is given to cornice detail, brick and stone accents or other finish items that make your home distinctive.

*House Cross-Sections*

*Detailed Floor Plans*

*Exterior Elevations*

*Interior Elevations*

*Foundation Plans*

*Frontal Sheet*

# *Important Extras To Do The Job Right!*

*Introducing seven important planning and construction aids developed by our professionals to help you succeed in your home-building project.*

## To Order, Call Toll Free 1-800-521-6797

To add these important extras to your Blueprint Package, simply indicate your choices on the order form on page 221 or call us Toll Free 1-800-521-6797 and we'll tell you more about these exciting products.

. . . . . . . . . . . . . . . . . . . . . . . .

## MATERIALS LIST

For many of the designs in our portfolio we offer a customized materials take-off that is invaluable in planning and estimating the cost of your new home. This comprehensive list outlines the quantity, type and size of material needed to build your house (with the exception of mechanical system items). Included are:

- framing lumber
- roofing and sheet metal
- windows and doors
- exterior sheathing material and trim
- masonry, veneer and fireplace materials
- tile and flooring materials
- kitchen and bath cabinetry
- interior drywall and trim
- rough and finish hardware
- many more items

(Note: Because of differing local codes, building methods, and availability of materials, our Materials Lists do not include mechanical materials. To obtain necessary take-offs and recommendations, consult heating, plumbing and electrical contractors. Materials Lists are not sold separately from the Blueprint Package.)

This handy list helps you or your builder cost out materials and serves as a ready reference sheet when you're compiling bids. It also provides a cross-check against the materials specified by your builder and helps coordinate the substitution of items you may need to meet local codes.

## SPECIFICATION OUTLINE

This valuable 16-page document is critical to building your house correctly. Designed to be filled in by you or your builder, this booklet lists 166 stages or items crucial to the building process.

For the layman, it provides a comprehensive review of the construction process and helps in making the specific choices of materials, models and processes. For the builder, it serves as a guide to preparing a building quotation and forms the basis for the construction program.

Designed primarily as a reference for the homeowner, this Specification Outline can become a legally binding document. Once it is filled out and agreed upon by owner and builder, it becomes a complete Project Specification.

When combined with the blueprints, a signed contract and schedule, the Specification Outline becomes a legal document and record for the building of your home. Many home builders find it useful to order two of these outlines—one as a worksheet in formulating the specifications and another to be carefully completed as a legal document.

## DETAIL SHEETS

If you want to know more about techniques—and deal more confidently with subcontractors—we offer these remarkably useful detail sheets. Each is an excellent tool that will enhance your understanding of these technical subjects.

# Plan-A-Home®

## PLUMBING

The Blueprint Package includes locations for all the plumbing fixtures in your new house, including sinks, lavatories, tubs, showers, toilets, laundry trays and water heaters. However, if you want to know more about the complete plumbing system, these 24x36-inch detail sheets will prove very useful. Prepared to meet requirements of the National Plumbing Code, these six fact-filled sheets give general information on pipe schedules, fittings, sump-pump details, water-softener hookups, septic system details and much more. Color-coded sheets include a glossary of terms.

## ELECTRICAL

The locations for every electrical switch, plug and outlet are shown in your Blueprint Package. However, these Electrical Details go further to take the mystery out of household electrical systems. Prepared to meet requirements of the National Electrical Code, these comprehensive 24x36-inch drawings come packed with helpful information, including wire sizing, switch-installation schematics, cable-routing details, appliance wattage, door-bell hook-ups, typical service panel circuitry and much more. Six sheets are bound together and color-coded for easy reference. A glossary of terms is also included.

Plan-A-Home® is an easy-to-use tool that helps you design a new home, arrange furniture in a new or existing home, or plan a remodeling project. Each package contains:

- More than *700 peel-off planning symbols* on a self-stick vinyl sheet, including walls, windows, doors, all types of furniture, kitchen components, bath fixtures and many more. All are made of durable, peel-and-stick vinyl you can use over and over.

- A reusable, transparent, *1/4-inch scale planning grid* made of tough mylar that matches the scale of actual working drawings (1/4 -inch equals 1 foot). This grid provides the basis for house layouts of up to 140x92 feet.

- *Tracing paper* and a protective sheet for copying or transferring your completed plan.

- A *felt-tip pen*, with water-soluble ink that wipes away quickly.

With Plan-A-Home®, you can make basic planning decisions for a new house or make modifications to an existing house. Use with your Blueprint Package to test modifications to rooms or to plan furniture arrangements before you build. Plan-A-Home® lets you lay out areas as large as a 7,500 square foot, six-bedroom, seven-bath house.

## CONSTRUCTION

The Blueprint Package contains everything an experienced builder needs to construct a particular house. However, it doesn't show all the ways that houses can be built, nor does it explain alternate construction methods. To help you understand how your house will be built—and offer additional techniques—this set of drawings depicts the materials and methods used to build foundations, fireplaces, walls, floors and roofs. Where appropriate, the drawings show acceptable alternatives. These six sheets will answer questions for the advanced do-it-yourselfer or home planner.

## MECHANICAL

This package contains fundamental principles and useful data that will help you make informed decisions and communicate with subcontractors about heating and cooling systems. The 24 x 36-inch drawings contain instructions and samples that allow you to make simple load calculations and preliminary sizing and costing analysis. Covered are today's most commonly used systems from heat pumps to solar fuel systems. The package is packed full of illustrations and diagrams to help you visualize components and how they relate to one another.

# House Blueprint Price Schedule and Plans Index

These pages contain all the information you need to price your blueprints. In general the larger and more complicated the house, the more it costs to design and thus the higher the price we must charge for the blueprints. Remember, however, that these prices are far less than you would normally pay for the services of a licensed architect or professional designer. Custom home designs and related architectural services often cost thousands of dollars, ranging from 5% to 15% of the cost of construction. By ordering our blueprints you are potentially saving enough money to afford a larger house, or to add those "extra" amenities such as a patio, deck, swimming pool or even an upgraded kitchen or luxurious master suite.

To use the Index below, refer to the design number listed in numerical order (a helpful page reference is also given). Note the price index letter and refer to the House Blueprint Price Schedule at right for the cost of one, four or eight sets of blueprints or the cost of a reproducible sepia. Additional prices are shown for identical and reverse blueprint sets, as well as a very useful Materials List for some of the plans.

## House Blueprint Price Schedule
(Prices guaranteed through December 31, 1995)

| | 1-set Study Package | 4-set Building Package | 8-set Building Package | 1-set Reproducible Sepias |
|---|---|---|---|---|
| Schedule A | $240 | $300 | $360 | $460 |
| Schedule B | $280 | $340 | $400 | $520 |
| Schedule C | $320 | $380 | $440 | $580 |
| Schedule D | $360 | $420 | $480 | $640 |
| Schedule E | $480 | $540 | $600 | $700 |

Additional Identical Blueprints in same order ................................................................$50 per set
Reverse Blueprints (mirror image) ................................................................................$50 per set
Specification Outlines................................................................................................$10 each
Materials Lists (for Home Planners', Design Basics', Alan Mascord's, and Donald Gardner's Plans only):
   ▲ Home Planners' Designs
       Schedule A-D ................................................................................................$40
       Schedule E ..................................................................................................$50
   † Design Basics' Designs................................................................................$75
   ◆ Donald Gardner's Designs ........................................................................$40
   ✳ Alan Mascord's Designs ............................................................................$40
Exchanges.........................$50 exchange fee for the first set; $10 for each additional set
                 $70 total exchange fee for 4 sets
                 $100 total exchange fee for 8 sets

**To Order:** Fill in and send the Order Form on page 221—or call us at 1-800-521-6797 or 1-602-297-8200.

# *Before You Order . . .*

Before completing the coupon at right or calling us on our Toll-Free Blueprint Hotline, you may be interested to learn more about our service and products. Here's some information you will find helpful.

## Quick Turnaround

We process and ship every blueprint order from our office within 48 hours. On most orders, we do even better. Normally, if we receive your order by 5 p.m. Eastern Time, we'll process it the same day and ship it the following day. Because of this quick turnaround, we won't send a formal notice acknowledging receipt of your order.

## Our Exchange Policy

Since blueprints are printed in response to your order, we cannot honor requests for refunds. However, we will exchange your entire first order for an equal number of blueprints plus the following exchange fees: $50 for the first set, $10 for each additional set; $70 total exchange fee for 4 sets; $100 total exchange fee for 8 sets.... *plus* the difference in cost if exchanging for a design in a higher price bracket, or *less* the difference in cost if exchanging for a design in a lower price bracket. (Sepias are not exchangeable.) All sets from the first order must be returned before the exchange can take place. Please add $10 for postage and handling via ground service; $20 via 2nd Day Air.

## About Reverse Blueprints

If you want to build in reverse of the plan as shown, we will include an extra set of reversed blueprints (mirror image) for an additional fee of $50. Although lettering and dimensions appear backward, reverses will be a useful visual aid if you decide to flop the plan.

## Modifying Our Plans

With such a great selection of homes, you are bound to find the one that suits you. However, if you need to make changes to the plans you have chosen, it may be easy for us to do this for you. Please ask for additional information when you place your order.

If you decide to revise plans significantly that are not customizable, we strongly suggest that you order reproducible sepias and consult a licensed architect or professional designer to help you redraw the plans.

## Architectural and Engineering Seals

Some cities and states are now requiring that a licensed architect or engineer review and "seal" your blueprints prior to construction. This is often due to local or regional concerns over energy consumption, safety codes, seismic ratings, etc. For this reason, you may find it necessary to consult with a local professional to have your plans reviewed. This can normally be accomplished with minimum delays, for a nominal fee.

## Compliance with Local Codes and Regulations

At the time of creation, our plans are drawn to specifications published by Building Officials Code Administrators (BOCA), the Southern Standard Building Code, or the Uniform Building Code and are designed to meet or exceed national building standards. Some states, counties and municipalities have their own codes, zoning requirements and building regulations. Before starting construction, consult with local building authorities and make sure you comply with local ordinances and codes, including obtaining any necessary permits or inspections as building progresses. In some cases, minor modifications to your plans by your builder, local architect or designer may be required to meet local conditions and requirements.

## Foundation and Exterior Wall Changes

Most of our plans are drawn with either a full or partial basement foundation. Depending upon your specific climate or regional building practices, you may wish to convert this basement to a slab or crawlspace. Most professional contractors and builders can easily adapt your plans to alternate foundation types. Likewise, most can easily convert 2x4 wall construction to 2x6, or vice versa. If you need more guidance on these conversions, our handy Construction Detail Sheets, shown on page 217, describe how such conversions can be made.

## How Many Blueprints Do You Need?

A single set of blueprints is sufficient to study a home in greater detail. However, if you are planning to obtain cost estimates from a contractor or subcontractors—or if you are planning to build immediately—you will need more sets. Because additional sets are cheaper when ordered in quantity with the original order, make sure you order enough blueprints to satisfy all requirements. The following checklist will help you determine how many you need:

_____Owner

_____Builder (generally requires at least three sets; one as a legal document, one to use during inspections, and at least one to give to subcontractors)

_____Local Building Department (often requires two sets)

_____Mortgage Lender (usually one set for a conventional loan; three sets for FHA or VA loans)

_____TOTAL NUMBER OF SETS

### Toll Free 1-800-521-6797

Normal Office Hours:
8:00 a.m. to 8:00 p.m. Eastern Time
Monday through Friday
Our staff will gladly answer any questions during normal office hours. Our answering service can place orders after hours or on weekends.

If we receive your order by 4:00 p.m. Eastern, Time, Monday through Friday, we'll process it the same day and ship it the following business day. When ordering by phone, please have your charge card ready. We'll also ask you for the Order Form Key Number at the bottom of the coupon. Please use our Toll-Free number for blueprint and book orders only.

By FAX: Copy the Order Form on the next page and send it on our FAX line: 1-800-224-6699 or 1-602-297-9937.

## Canadian Customers
### Order Toll-Free 1-800-848-2550

For faster, more economical service, Canadian customers may now call in orders on our Toll-Free line. Or, complete the order form at right, adding 30% to all prices and mail in Canadian funds to:

**Home Planners, Inc.**
3275 W. Ina Road, Suite 110
Tucson, AZ 85741

By FAX: Copy the Order Form on the next page and send it on our FAX line: 1-800-224-6699 or 1-602-297-9937.

# O R D E R   F O R M

**HOME PLANNERS, INC., 3275 WEST INA ROAD**
SUITE 110, TUCSON, ARIZONA 85741

**BASIC BLUEPRINT PACKAGE**
me the following (please refer to the Plans Index and
Schedule in this section):

___ Set(s) of blueprints for plan number(s) _____. $_____
___ Set(s) of sepias for plan number(s) _____. $_____
___ Additional identical blueprints in same order
    @ $50.00 per set. $_____
___ Reverse blueprints @ $50.00 per set. $_____

**RTANT EXTRAS**
me the following:

___ Materials List: Home Planners' Designs @ $40 Schedule A-D;
    $50 Schedule E; $75 Design Basics' Designs; $40 Alan
    Mascord's Designs; $40 Donald Gardner's Designs. $_____
___ Specification Outlines @ $10.00 each. $_____
___ Detail Sets @ $14.95 each; any two for $22.95; any three
    for $29.95; all four for $39.95 (save $19.85). $_____
    ❑ Plumbing ❑ Electrical ❑ Construction ❑ Mechanical
    (These helpful details provide general construction
    advice and are not specific to any single plan.)
___ Plan-A-Home® @ $29.95 each. $_____

**-TOTAL** $_____

| POSTAGE AND DLING | 1-3 sets | 4 or more sets | |
|---|---|---|---|
| VERY (Requires street ss - No P.O. Boxes) | | | |
| lar Service w 4-6 days delivery | ❑ $8.00 | ❑ $10.00 | $_____ |
| Day Air w 2-3 days delivery | ❑ $12.00 | ❑ $20.00 | $_____ |
| Day Air w 1 day delivery | ❑ $22.00 | ❑ $30.00 | $_____ |
| OFFICE DELIVERY treet address available. 4-6 days delivery | ❑ $10.00 | ❑ $14.00 | $_____ |
| SEAS AIR MAIL VERY All delivery times are from lueprint Package is shipped. | Phone, Fax or Mail for quote | | |

**TAGE** (From above) $_____
**ES TAX** (Arizona residents add 5% sales tax; Michigan residents add 6% sales tax.) $_____
**AL (Sub-total, postage and tax)** $_____

**R ADDRESS (please print)**

___ _____
___ _____
___ _____State_____Zip _____
me telephone number (____) _____

**CREDIT CARD ORDERS ONLY**
e fill in the information below:

t card number _____
Date: Month/Year_____
one ❑ Visa ❑ MasterCard ❑ Discover Card
ture _____

Form Key    Please check appropriate box:
[B26BP]    ❑ Licensed Builder-Contractor
           ❑ Home Owner

☎ **ORDER TOLL FREE**
**1-800-521-6797**
or
**1-602-297-8200**

**UEPRINTS ARE NOT RETURNABLE**

# O R D E R   F O R M

**HOME PLANNERS, INC., 3275 WEST INA ROAD**
SUITE 110, TUCSON, ARIZONA 85741

**THE BASIC BLUEPRINT PACKAGE**
Rush me the following (please refer to the Plans Index and
Price Schedule in this section):

___ Set(s) of blueprints for plan number(s) _____. $_____
___ Set(s) of sepias for plan number(s) _____. $_____
___ Additional identical blueprints in same order
    @ $50.00 per set. $_____
___ Reverse blueprints @ $50.00 per set. $_____

**IMPORTANT EXTRAS**
Rush me the following:

___ Materials List: Home Planners' Designs @ $40 Schedule A-D;
    $50 Schedule E; $75 Design Basics' Designs; $40 Alan
    Mascord's Designs; $40 Donald Gardner's Designs. $_____
___ Specification Outlines @ $10.00 each. $_____
___ Detail Sets @ $14.95 each; any two for $22.95; any three
    for $29.95; all four for $39.95 (save $19.85). $_____
    ❑ Plumbing ❑ Electrical ❑ Construction ❑ Mechanical
    (These helpful details provide general construction
    advice and are not specific to any single plan.)
___ Plan-A-Home® @ $29.95 each. $_____

**SUB-TOTAL** $_____

| POSTAGE AND HANDLING | 1-3 sets | 4 or more sets | |
|---|---|---|---|
| **DELIVERY** (Requires street address - No P.O. Boxes) | | | |
| •Regular Service Allow 4-6 days delivery | ❑ $8.00 | ❑ $10.00 | $_____ |
| •2nd Day Air Allow 2-3 days delivery | ❑ $12.00 | ❑ $20.00 | $_____ |
| •Next Day Air Allow 1 day delivery | ❑ $22.00 | ❑ $30.00 | $_____ |
| **POST OFFICE DELIVERY** If no street address available. Allow 4-6 days delivery | ❑ $10.00 | ❑ $14.00 | $_____ |
| **OVERSEAS AIR MAIL DELIVERY** Note: All delivery times are from date Blueprint Package is shipped. | Phone, Fax or Mail for quote | | |

**POSTAGE** (From above) $_____
**SALES TAX** (Arizona residents add 5% sales tax; Michigan residents add 6% sales tax.) $_____
**TOTAL (Sub-total, postage and tax)** $_____

**YOUR ADDRESS (please print)**

Name _____
Street _____
City _____State_____Zip _____
Daytime telephone number (____) _____

**FOR CREDIT CARD ORDERS ONLY**
Please fill in the information below:

Credit card number _____
Exp. Date: Month/Year_____
Check one ❑ Visa ❑ MasterCard ❑ Discover Card
Signature _____

Order Form Key    Please check appropriate box:
[TB26BP]    ❑ Licensed Builder-Contractor
            ❑ Home Owner

☎ **ORDER TOLL FREE**
**1-800-521-6797**
or
**1-602-297-8200**

**BLUEPRINTS ARE NOT RETURNABLE**

# Additional Plans Books

**1. ENCYCLOPEDIA OF HOME DESIGNS (EN)** Our best collection of plans is now bigger and better than ever! Over 500 plans organized by architectural category. Includes all types and styles. The most comprehensive plan book ever. 352 pages. $9.95 ($12.95 Can.)

**2. THE ESSENTIAL GUIDE TO TRADITIONAL HOMES (ET)** Over 400 traditional homes in one special volume. American and European styles from Farmhouses to Norman French. Best sellers shown in color photographs and renderings. 304 pages. $9.95 ($12.95 Can.)

**3. THE ESSENTIAL GUIDE TO CONTEMPORARY HOMES (EC)** More than 340 contemporary designs from Northwest Contemporary to Post-Modern Victorian. Color section of best sellers; two-color illustrations throughout. 304 pages. $9.95 ($12.95 Can.)

**4. AFFORDABLE HOME PLANS (AH)** For the prospective home builder with a modest or medium budget. Features 430 one-, 1½-, two-story and multi-level homes in a wealth of styles. Cost-saving ideas for the budget-conscious included. 320 pages. $8.95 ($11.95 Can.)

**5. LUXURY DREAM HOMES (LD2)** New Edition! Completely updated with 50% new designs, this exciting collection of 154 designs now contains the home you've been waiting for! 192 pages. $14.95 ($18.95 Can.)

**6. ONE-STORY HOMES (V1)** A collection of 470 homes to suit a range of budgets in one-story living. All popular styles including Cape Cod, Southwestern, Tudor and French. 384 pages. $8.95 ($11.95 Can.)

**7. TWO-STORY HOMES (V2)** 478 plans for all budgets in a wealth of styles: Tudors, Saltboxes, Farmhouses, Victorians, Georgians, Contemporaries and more. 416 pages. $8.95 ($11.95 Can.)

**8. MULTI-LEVEL AND HILLSIDE HOMES (V3)** 312 distinctive styles for both flat and sloping sites. Includes exposed lower levels, open staircases, balconies, decks and terraces. 320 pages. $6.95 ($9.95 Can.)

**9. VACATION AND SECOND HOMES (V4)** 258 ideal plans for a favorite vacation spot or perfect retirement or starter home. Includes cottages, chalets and one-, 1½-, two-story, and multi-level homes. 256 pages. $5.95 ($7.95 Can.)

**10. STARTER HOMES (ST)** 200 easy-to-build plans—from simple do-it-yourself houses to more stylish contemporary designs. Features the all-new Economy Building Series. 224 pages. $6.95 ($9.95 Can.)

**11. EMPTY-NESTER HOMES (EP)** Perfect for empty-nesters, retirees and couples without children. These 206 plans feature sophisticated designs and upgraded amenities. 224 pages. $6.95 ($9.95 Can.)

**12. 200 FAMILY-FAVORED HOME PLANS (FF)** Expanded designs for expanding families! Seven top designers present move-up home combining beautiful styling with more living space. 224 pages. $7.95 ($10.95 Can.)

**13. 200 NARROW-LOT HOME PLANS (NL)** The largest collection ever of homes that meet the unique challenges of today's narrow lots. Up to 3,000 square feet at less than 60-ft. widths! 224 pages. $7.95 ($10.95 Can.)

**14. 200 FARMHOUSE AND COUNTRY HOME PLANS (FH)** Styles and sizes to match every taste and budget, from Classic Farmhouses to Country Capes and Cottages. Expertly drawn floor plans and renderings enhance the sections. 224 pages. $7.95 ($10.95 Can.)

**15. 200 BUDGET-SMART HOME PLANS (BS)** The definitive source for the home builder with a limited budget—have your home and enjoy it too! Amenity-laden homes, in many sizes and styles, can all be built from our plans. 224 pages. $7.95 ($10.95 Can.)

**16. MOST POPULAR HOME DESIGNS (MP)** 400 of our customers' favorites! One-story, 1½-story, two-story and multi-level homes in a variety of styles. Designs feature-laden with lounges, clutter rooms, media rooms and more. 304 pages. $9.95 ($12.95 Can.)

**17. NEW ENGLAND SAMPLER (NES)** New England architecture—inside and out! 264 Cape Cods, Saltboxes, Garrisons, Georgians and other Colonial classics—many developed for *Colonial Homes* magazine. 200 interior illustrations included. 384 pages. $14.95 ($18.95 Can.)

**18. VICTORIAN DREAM HOMES (VDH)** 160 Victorian and Farmhouse designs by three master designers. Victorian style from Second Empire homes through the Queen Anne and Folk Victorian era. Beautiful renderings with modern floor plans. 192 pages. $12.95 ($16.95 Can.)

**19. WESTERN HOME PLANS (WH)** Over 215 home plans from Spanish Mission and Monterey to Northwest Chateau and San Francisco Victorian. Historical notes trace the background and geographical incidence of each style. 208 pages. $8.95 ($11.95 Can.)

**20. THE HOME REMODELER (HR)** A revolutionary book of 31 remodeling plans backed by complete construction-ready blueprints and materials lists. Kitchens, baths, master bedrooms and much more. Ideas, advice, suggestions. 112 pages. $7.95 ($10.95 Can.)

**21. DECK PLANNER (DP)** 25 practical plans and details for decks the do-it-yourselfer can actually build. How-to data and project starters for a variety of decks. Construction details available separately. 112 pages. $7.95 ($10.95 Can.)

**22. THE HOME LANDSCAPER (HL)** 55 fabulous front and backyard plans that even the do-it-yourselfer can master. Complete construction blueprints and regionalized plant lists available for each design. 208 pages. $12.95 ($16.95 Can.)

☎ **TO ORDER BOOKS BY PHONE**
**1-800-322-6797**

**CANADIAN CUSTOMERS:** Order books toll-free: 1-800-561-4169. Or, complete this form, using Canadian prices and adding postage, and mail with Canadian funds to: The Plan Centre, 20 Cedar Street North, Kitchener Ont. N2H 2W8. FAX: 1-519-743-1282.

**23. THE BACKYARD LANDSCAPER (BYL)** Sequel to *The Home Landscaper,* contains 40 professionally designed plans for backyards. Do yourself or contract out. Complete construction blueprints and regionalized plant lists available. 160 pages. $12.95 ($16.95 Can.)

- - - - - - - - - - - - - - - - - - - - - - - - - - - - - - - - - - -

# Additional Books Order Form

To order your Home Planners books, just check the box of the book numbered below and complete the coupon. We will process your order and ship it from our office within 48 hours. Send coupon and check (in U.S. funds) to: Home Planners, Inc, 3275 W. Ina Rd., Ste.110, Dept. BK, Tucson, AZ 85741

**ES!** Please send me the design books I've indicated:

1: Encyclopedia of Home Designs (EN) .......................$9.95 ($12.95 Can.)
2: 403 Traditional Home Plans (ET) ..............................$9.95 ($12.95 Can.)
3: 340 Contemporary Home Plans (EC) ......................$9.95 ($12.95 Can.)
4: Affordable Home Plans (AH) ...................................$8.95 ($11.95 Can.)
5: Luxury Dream Homes (LD2) ...................................$14.95 ($18.95 Can.)
6: One-Story Homes (V1) ...........................................$8.95 ($11.95 Can.)
7: Two-Story Homes (V2) ...........................................$8.95 ($11.95 Can.)
8: Multi-Level & Hillside Homes (V3) ...........................$6.95 ($9.95 Can.)
9: Vacation & Second Homes (V4) ..............................$5.95 ($7.95 Can.)
0: Starter Homes (ST) .................................................$6.95 ($9.95 Can.)
1: Empty-Nester Homes (EP) ......................................$6.95 ($9.95 Can.)
2: 200 Family-Favored Home Plans (FF) ....................$7.95 ($10.95 Can.)
3: 200 Narrow-Lot Home Plans (NL) ...........................$7.95 ($10.95 Can.)
4: 200 Farmhouse & Country Home Plans (FH) ...........$7.95 ($10.95 Can.)
5: 200 Budget-Smart Home Plans (BS) .......................$7.95 ($10.95 Can.)
6: 400 Most Popular Home Designs (MP) .....................$9.95 ($12.95 Can.)
7: New England Sampler (NES) ..................................$14.95 ($18.95 Can.)
8: Victorian Dream Homes (VDH) ...............................$12.95 ($16.95 Can.)
9: Western Home Plans (WH) .....................................$8.95 ($11.95 Can.)
0: The Home Remodeler (HR) .....................................$7.95 ($10.95 Can.)
1: Deck Planner (DP) ..................................................$7.95 ($10.95 Can.)
2: The Home Landscaper (HL) ....................................$12.95 ($16.95 Can.)
3: The Backyard Landscaper (BYL) .............................$12.95 ($16.95 Can.)

 **Home Planners, Inc.**
3275 W Ina Road, Suite 110, Dept. BK, Tucson, AZ 85741

Additional Books Sub-Total                                              $_____
Ariz. residents add 5% Sales Tax; Mich. residents
add 6% Sales Tax                                                              $_____
ADD Postage and Handling                                              $   3.00
YOUR TOTAL (Sub-Total, Tax, Postage/Handling)       $_____

**YOUR ADDRESS** (Please print)

Name _____

Street _____

City _____ State _____ Zip _____

Phone (_____) _____—_____

**YOUR PAYMENT**
Check one: ☐ Check  ☐ Visa  ☐ MasterCard  ☐ Discover Card
Required credit card information:

Credit Card Number _____

Expiration Date (Month/Year)_____/ _____

Signature Required_____

TB26 BK

223

*Design Q9621*

# OVER 3 MILLION BLUEPRINTS SOLD

*"We instructed our builder to follow the plans including all of the many details which make this house so elegant... Our home is a fine example of the results one can achieve by purchasing and following the plans which you offer... Everyone who has seen it has assured us that it belongs in 'a picture book.' I truly mean it when I say that my home 'is a DREAM HOUSE.'"*

S.P.
Anderson, SC

*"We have had a steady stream of visitors, many of whom tell us this is the most beautiful home they've seen. Everyone is amazed at the layout and remarks on how unique it is. Our real estate attorney, who is a Chicago dweller and who deals with highly valued properties, told me this is the only suburban home he has seen that he would want to live in."*

W. & P.S.
Flossmoor, IL

*"Your blueprints saved us a great deal of money. I acted as the general contractor and we did a lot of the work ourselves. We probably built it for half the cost! We are thinking about more plans for another home. I purchased a competitor's book but my husband wants only your plans!"*

K.M.
Grovetown, GA

*"We are very happy with the product of our efforts. The neighbors and passersby appreciate what we have created. We have had many people stop by to discuss our house and kindly praise it as being the nicest house in our area of new construction. We have even had one person stop and make us an unsolicited offer to buy the house for much more than we have invested in it."*

K. & L.S.
Bolingbrook, IL

*"The traffic going past our house is unbelievable. On several occasions, we have heard that it is the 'prettiest house in Batvia.' Also, when meeting someone new and mentioning what street we live on, quite often we're told, 'Oh, you're the one in the yellow house with the wrap-around porch! I love it!'"*

A.W.
Batvia, NY

*"I have been involved in the building trades my entire life... Since building our home we have built two other homes for other families. Their plans from local professional architects were not nearly as good as yours. For that reason we are ordering additional plan books from you."*

T.F.
Kingston, WA

*"The blueprints we received from you were of excellent quality and provided us with exactly what we needed to get our successful home-building project underway. We appreciate your invaluable role in our home-building effort."*

T.A.
Concord, TN